History According to SAT

A Content Guide to SAT Reading and Writing

Elizabeth Breau, Ph.D.

History According to SAT: A Content Guide to SAT Reading and Writing
© 2022, Elizabeth Breau, Ph.D. All rights reserved.
Published by Prep for Success, LLC, Highland Park, New Jersey

Print ISBN: 979-8-9860291-0-8
Ebook ISBN: 979-8-9860291-1-5
Library of Congress Control Number: 2022907805

Website | www.elizabethbreau.net

SAT™ *is a trademark registered by the College Board, which is not affiliated with, and does not endorse, this publication.*

This book is intended to provide accurate information with regard to its subject matter and reflects the opinion and perspective of the author. However, in times of rapid change, ensuring all information provided is entirely accurate and up-to-date at all times is not always possible. Therefore, the author and publisher accept no responsibility for inaccuracies or omissions and specifically disclaim any liability, loss or risk, personal, professional or otherwise, which may be incurred as a consequence, directly or indirectly, of the use and/or application of any of the contents of this book.

To my mother, Miriam Breau (1942–2000).

WHAT REVIEWERS ARE SAYING

A seasoned SAT prep instructor... Breau "does not discuss test-taking strategies or tricks for making educated guesses." Instead she distills more than a millennium of world history from the Middle Ages through the 1990s into a concise narrative of fewer than 300 pages that highlights "the historical context of documents and speeches that appear frequently as test passages." ...this book succeeds in its goal of helping students navigate a flawed educational paradigm.

– Kirkus Reviews

The SAT reading comprehension questions often assume that students know a core set of western cultural and historical information. From years of prepping students for the exam, Dr. Elizabeth Breau knows this isn't always the case, often through no fault of the students themselves. This book helps students close that bias gap with succinct and engaging essays providing the historical context students need to perform well on the SAT. Nearly every student (and likely their parents as well) would benefit from reading it.

– Erik Bledsoe, former Lecturer in English and
American Studies, University of Tennessee

I've been helping students prepare for the SAT for 15 years, and my students have struggled most with the historical passages. In *History According to SAT*, Dr. Breau presents world and American history relevant to the SAT in an easy-to-read format that incorporates vocabulary words and definitions, technological and philosophical trends, and interconnections among global events. The format works very well: historical narrative integrated with bullet-point lists of key events, people, laws, and inventions. Other great elements include the immediate explanations of complicated terms and well-placed illustrations. In addition, Dr. Breau explains many historical writings that have appeared on previous SATs and identifies similar writings that are likely to appear on future tests. I look forward to using this resource to supplement my students' preparation.

– *Bridget Heneghan, Ph.D.*

CONTENTS

INTRODUCTION 1

A Note for Parents and Teachers 1
SAT Basics 3
How This Book Will Help You 4
My Sources 5
Telling the "Story" of History 5
Making Quick Sense of History 6
A Note about Historical Time 7

PART I: THE MIDDLE AGES THROUGH WORLD WAR II 9

The Middle Ages (500–1500) 9

The Catholic Church 9
Divine Right of Kings 10
Feudalism 11
Chivalry 11
Ottoman Empire 11
Spanish Inquisition 12
United Kingdom 14

The Renaissance (1300–1600) 19

Bubonic Plague 19
Asian Influences on Europe 20
Reason 21
Niccolò Machiavelli 21
Renaissance Women 22
Renaissance Inventions 23
Renaissance Music 24
Renaissance Art 25
Protestant Reformation 27
Age of Exploration 31
Race-Based Slavery 32
Pilgrims 33

The Enlightenment (1685–1815) 37

Social Contract 38
Glorious Revolution 38
Enlightenment Thinkers 39

The American Revolution (1765–1783) 41

French and Indian War 41
Tensions Rise in the American
Colonies 42
Boston Massacre 43
Boston Tea Party 43
First Continental Congress 45

Patrick Henry 45
Paul Revere's Ride 45
Second Continental Congress 46
Battle of Bunker Hill 46
Declaration of Independence 46
Thomas Paine 47
Washington Crosses the Delaware 47
Battle of Saratoga 48

Winter at Valley Forge 48
American Allies 49
Battle of Yorktown 49
Treaty of Paris 50
Constitutional Convention 50
Three-Fifths Compromise 50
United States Constitution 51

The Industrial Revolution (1760–1840)   53

Inventions 53
Adam Smith 58

Transcendentalism 60

The French Revolution (1789–1799)   61

A Brief History of France 61
Storming of the Bastille 65
Declaration of the Rights of Man 65

Women's March on Versailles 66
Reign of Terror 66
Haitian Revolution 67

Nineteenth-Century Europe (1800–1914)   69

Napoleonic Wars 69
European Peace 70
Economic Disruption 71
Russia 72
Marxism 73

Irish Potato Famine 74
Revolutions of 1848 75
Crimean War 76
Boer Wars 77

Nineteenth-Century United States (1800–1860)   78

War of 1812 78
Monroe Doctrine 79
Alexis de Tocqueville 80
Indian Removal Act 81
Texan Independence 81
Mexican-American War 83
Prelude to Civil War 84
Mason-Dixon Line 85
Fugitive Slave Acts 85
Missouri Compromise 86
Underground Railroad 86

Harriet Tubman 87
Missouri Compromise of 1850 87
Bleeding Kansas 88
Pottawatomie Massacre 90
Dred Scott v. Sandford 90
Lincoln-Douglas Debates 90
Raid on Harpers Ferry 90
Abolitionist Literature 91
African American Newspapers 91
White Abolitionists' Writings 92

The American Civil War (1860–1865)   93

Southern Secession 93
Battles of Bull Run 96
Battle of Antietam 96
Emancipation Proclamation 96
First Conscription Act 97
Battle of Gettysburg 97

Siege of Vicksburg 98
New York Draft Riots 98
Gettysburg Address 99
Sherman's March 101
Confederate Army Surrenders 102
Lincoln's Assassination 102

United States (1865–1914)　　　　　　103

Reconstruction 103
Forty Acres and a Mule 104
President Andrew Johnson 104
Thirteenth Amendment 105
Fourteenth Amendment 106
Fifteenth Amendment 106
Sharecropping 106
Plessy v. Ferguson 107
Immigration 108
Chinese Exclusion Act 109
Women's Rights 110
Second Industrial Revolution 112

Gilded Age 113
Progressive Era 113
Solutions to Urban Poverty 114
Muckraking 115
African American Progressives 116
Temperance Movement 118
Labor Movement 119
Pinkerton Detective Agency 120
Homestead Strike 120
Pullman Strike 121
Triangle Shirtwaist Factory Fire 122
Spanish-American War 122

World War I (1914–1918)　　　　　　123

European Geopolitics 124
Assassination of Archduke Franz
　　Ferdinand 124
War Begins 125
Submarine Warfare 126
Sinking of the *Lusitania* 127

Zimmerman Telegram 127
Women in Wartime 130
Treaty of Versailles 130
Russian Revolution of 1917 132
Russian Civil War 132

United States (1919–1929)　　　　　　133

First Red Scare 133
Race and Racism 134
Black Wall Street 134
Great Migration 135
Harlem Renaissance 136
Women's Suffrage 137

Influenza Epidemic 138
Prohibition 139
Roaring Twenties 139
Art Deco 141
Laissez-Faire Economics 141

Europe in the 1920s　　　　　　142

Fascism 142

National Socialist German Workers'
　　(NAZI) Party 144

Great Depression (1929–1939)　　　　　　145

Stock Market 145
Stock Market Crash of 1929 146
Dust Bowl 147
President Franklin D. Roosevelt 148

Fireside Chats 148
Works Progress Administration 149
Great Depression in Europe 149

World War II (1939–1945)　　　　　　152

Invasion of Poland 152
Blitzkrieg 153
Miracle at Dunkirk 154
Winston Churchill 155
Battle of Britain 156
Vichy France 156

Operation Barbarossa 156
Japan (1929–1939) 157
Attack on Pearl Harbor 158
United States Mobilizes for War 159
Battle of Attu 159
Bataan Death March 160

Battle of Midway 160
Home Front 160
Internment of Japanese
   Americans 161
Women During World War II 163
Segregation in the United States
   Armed Forces 164
Tuskegee Airmen 165

Double V for Victory 166
Navajo Code Talkers 167
North African Campaign 168
Italy Drops Out 168
D-Day 169
Battle of the Bulge 170
Atomic Bomb 171
Holocaust and Other Atrocities 172

PART II: THE POSTWAR ERA (1945–1990)   175

Postcolonialism   175

United Nations 176
Indian Independence 176
Mohandas Gandhi 176
Partition of India and Pakistan 177
Israeli Statehood 179
Palestine 179
Zionism 180
Suez Canal 181

McMahon-Hussein Agreement 181
Sykes-Picot Agreement 181
Balfour Declaration 181
Jewish Refugees 183
First Arab-Israeli War 185
Six-Day War 185
Fourth Arab-Israeli War 187
Camp David Accords 187

Cold War (1947–1991)   188

Cold War Basics 189
The Iron Curtain Falls 191
Eleanor Roosevelt 192
Containment 192
Truman Doctrine 193
Domino Theory 193
Marshall Plan 194
Berlin Airlift 194
North Atlantic Treaty Organization
   (NATO) 194
Nuclear Arms Race 195
Second Red Scare 196
Military-Industrial Complex 198
Berlin Wall 198
Nonaligned Nations 199
Space Race 199
Cuban Revolution 200
Bay of Pigs Invasion 201
Cuban Missile Crisis 202

Assassination of President
   Kennedy 202
Chinese Communist Revolution 203
Korean War 204
Vietnam War 205
Gulf of Tonkin 207
Operation Rolling Thunder 209
Tet Offensive 209
My Lai Massacre 209
Tallying the Dead 210
Nixon's Vietnam Policy 210
Pentagon Papers 211
Nixon Goes to China 212
Watergate Scandal 212
Fall of Saigon 213
Cambodian Civil War 214
Cambodian Genocide 214
Indochina Refugee Crisis 215

Civil Rights Movements   215

Brown v. Board of Education 216
Little Rock Nine 217
Murder of Emmett Till 217

Montgomery Bus Boycott 218
Dr. Martin Luther King, Jr 218
Browder v. Gale 219

Freedom Rides 219
Birmingham Campaign 220
Birmingham Church Bombing 221
March on Washington for Jobs and
    Freedom 222
John Lewis 222
Murder of Medgar Evers 223
Freedom Summer 223
Civil Rights Act of 1964 224
Selma-to-Montgomery March 224
Voting Rights Act 225
Malcolm X 226
Student Nonviolent Coordinating
    Committee (SNCC) 227

Black Power Movement 228
1967 Race Riots 229
Assassination of Martin Luther
    King, Jr. 230
Robert F. Kennedy 230
Second-Wave Feminism 230
Title VII 232
Title IX 232
Native American Rights
    Movement.. 232
Indian Relocation Act 233
Trail of Broken Treaties 233
Chicano Rights 234
Gay Rights Movement 234

End of Cold War (1980–1991)   236

Soviet Union Invades Afghanistan ... 236
Reagan Doctrine 237
Changes in the Soviet Union 237
Fall of the Berlin Wall 238

Poland and the Solidarity
    Movement 239
Estonian Singing Revolution 239
August Coup 240

PART III: POST-COLD WAR TO THE END OF HISTORY ACCORDING TO SAT (1991–1995)   243

Globalization   243

South Africa and Apartheid   243

Defiance Campaign 245
Nelson Mandela 245
Sharpeville Massacre 246

Rivonia Trial 246
Soweto Youth Uprising 247
Divestment 248

HIV/AIDS   249

"Women's Rights are Human Rights"   253

CONCLUSION   254

IMAGE ATTRIBUTIONS   256

ACKNOWLEDGMENTS   259

ABOUT THE AUTHOR   260

INTRODUCTION

A Note for Parents and Teachers

Every two years, the National Assessment of Educational Progress issues the nation's educational report card, which is based on standardized tests in math and reading. The most recent report card is disheartening: only about one-third of American students read at grade level. This outcome is a direct result of a twenty-one-year-old educational reform initiative called "No Child Left Behind." This initiative ushered in an era of skills-based teaching, in which reading skills, such as decoding, phonics, and vocabulary, are taught in stand-alone units that subordinate content to skills practice.

However, there is now evidence that skills-based instruction is insufficient on its own. One study of third-graders, based on a reading passage about soccer, showed that poor readers who knew about soccer were able to make more accurate inferences about what they read than strong readers who knew nothing about the sport. Another study found that eleventh-graders with broad-based general knowledge (as measured by a standardized test) performed better on reading comprehension tests than students who did poorly on the same general knowledge test.

In my experience as a secondary school and test prep teacher, I have seen that many American high school students are unable to understand SAT READING passages even when they remember learning related material in school. They have a confused or incorrect sense of the order of historical events, so they misunderstand what they read. I have taught tenth-graders who told me that American slavery ended in 1945 at the end of World War II instead of in 1865 when the North defeated the South in the American Civil War. This misunderstanding could confuse students when they read a Reconstruction-era passage about civil rights for black people because they think the author is talking about people who are still enslaved. Other students have never heard of the French Revolution, so they misread multiple passages by the anti-revolutionary Edmund Burke, whose work frequently appears on SAT READING.

This book does not discuss test-taking strategies or tricks for making educated guesses when choosing answers. Instead, it explains the historical context of documents and speeches that appear frequently as test passages so that students can more easily understand what they say. For example, test passages have been taken from the United States Declaration of Independence. Students who are unfamiliar with its contents must labor through its complex sentences and high-level vocabulary without assistance, whereas those who have read and studied it are much better equipped to navigate those challenges during testing. Simply put, test passages are easier for students who already know the events and ideas those passages discuss than for those who do not.

SAT Basics

The SAT does not test students on specific knowledge. There is no national curriculum in the United States, so test designers cannot be sure that all students will have studied the same material. Instead, the test assesses how well students can perform a variety of reading and writing tasks, such as differentiating between main ideas and details, recognizing accurate restatements, selecting the best wording, inferring an author's opinion correctly, and deciding which word fits a sentence best.

The SAT READING test consists of five passages and fifty-two multiple-choice questions. One passage is usually "literature," which means that it is taken from a novel, short story, or memoir; the remaining four are usually some combination of history, science, and social science. One or two passages on each test will actually be a set of "paired passages" that both discuss the same topic but from different points of view.

Each SAT READING passage is followed by ten or eleven multiple-choice questions that require students to perform various reading comprehension skills: match the article's main point to an accurate restatement of the same ideas, select the example that best supports the author's main claim, and infer accurately or explain what an idiomatic expression means in the context of a given passage. Each set of questions also contains questions about vocabulary and questions that ask, "Which choice provides the best evidence for the answer to the previous question?"

SAT WRITING consists of four passages that are each followed by eleven multiple-choice questions that test students' knowledge of grammar, sentence mechanics, and vocabulary. The passages are not original documents and are written for general readers. They are often about historical figures or events: "firsts" in history, sports, science, and other fields; significant medical or technological discoveries and inventions; and the art, music, and cultures of different historical periods. The questions that accompany the passages are intended to be answered as students read, but questions that ask them about paragraph organization or appropriate transitions can require them to read a little ahead.

Introduction for Students: How this Book Will Help You

This book provides a brief overview of the background knowledge I draw on when I teach SAT READING and SAT WRITING. All of the information it contains is chosen because I have had to explain it to my SAT students. None of it is specialized or in-depth because SAT passages are selected from texts that are intended for general readers, not from texts written for experts.

1. This book provides a broad historical narrative that connects events in different times and places to each other.
2. It summarizes the content of important historical documents so that you can understand them if they appear on the test.
3. It explains important ideas and controversies and defines the vocabulary that people used to discuss these topics when they occurred.
4. It uses the text features listed below to streamline the reading experience, minimize confusion, and maximize your abilities to understand what you read on the SAT.
   a. In-Text Definitions: Whenever I use a word that students often don't know, I define it in parentheses immediately after it appears in the text for the first time, so it looks like this: "The dearth (lack) of rules led to total chaos."

b. Words, names, and phrases that require a longer explanation are marked with an asterisk (*) and are expanded directly below the paragraph in which they appear.

c. Keywords—important names and phrases—that students might encounter on the SAT are **stylized** the first time they appear so that they stand out on the page as **new information**. "New information" can include terms you might have learned in another context or that might help you make connections between different time periods and events.

d. Finally, the phrases SAT READING and SAT WRITING are gray and capitalized when they appear so that you will connect the test to what you are reading about.

My Sources

I have verified my dates, facts, and definitions on multiple free online resources: encyclopedias, museum websites, state park websites, presidential libraries, and state, federal, and military online archives. I used encyclopedias for kids and test prep websites to figure out what adults think students should know about various events. I was careful to avoid "political" websites, as well as those that respond to or interpret the news. My circle of readers, who are all smart, well-read history buffs, also double-checked my claims for accuracy.

Telling the "Story" of History

Writers use language to communicate both facts and interpretations of those facts that suggest relationships between them. For example, saying that Event A happened before Event B is different from saying that Event A *caused* Event B. Writers also use transition words that sometimes suggest that certain events or consequences were good or bad. For example, saying, "Unfortunately, 153 people died," has a different connotation (emotional meaning) than simply saying, "153 people died." The second sentence simply states a fact without giving it a positive or negative meaning.

I have done my best to avoid any language that suggests bias (opinion) and to state the facts without interpreting them. Whenever a topic or event is controversial (argued about), I explain the source of the controversy, the positions held by different sides of the argument, and how it was or was not resolved.

Making Quick Sense of History

You don't need to be a historian to understand historical passages on the SAT READING test. You don't need to memorize the names and dates of a zillion battles or be able to recite the names of the nineteenth-century American presidents in order. Instead, you need to understand the broad outlines of about seven hundred years of historical ideas and controversies so that they make sense to you when you see them out of context.

This is not as hard as it sounds. Significant historical events are connected to each other in multiple ways, and you are more likely to answer questions correctly if you understand how everything fits together.

This book provides an overview of the important events and ideas of American history from its pre-history in the Middle Ages to the year 1995—anything after that is too recent to count as "history." In general, SAT READING passages are taken from important documents and speeches that tell pieces of the story about how the idea of democracy—government by the people—developed, how the United States was created, and how those ideas have played out over time. If you know the context of what you are reading, you have a better chance of answering reading comprehension questions correctly.

Before we begin, however, I want to make clear that the history that will help you excel on the SAT is not all the history there is. It is only the history of how the United States came to exist as it does today. This limitation makes sense because the SAT is an American test. To tell that story, I've included the rough outlines of European and American history from the fourteenth century (1300s*) until 1995. It includes parts of the histories of Africa, Asia, and South and Central America, but only when events in those places affected the United States or the status of democracy in the world.

* The "first century" went from 0–99 AD, the second from 100–199, and so on.

A Note about Historical Time

Historians divide history into periods such as the Middle Ages, the Renaissance, or the Industrial Revolution for convenience, but the dates they attach to these periods are approximate and often overlap one another. Don't let this confuse you!

Let's get started!

PART I: THE MIDDLE AGES THROUGH WORLD WAR II

The Middle Ages (500–1500)

For about a thousand years, European life was characterized by **feudalism** (rule by kings and nobles), **chivalry** (a knightly code of honor), and a strong **Catholic Church***.

> * When spelled with a small "c," catholic means universal. When capitalized, it refers to the Catholic Church, headed by the Pope in Rome.

The Catholic Church: During the Middle Ages, the Catholic Church played a central role in the lives of Europeans, controlling how they lived and thought. Most people were illiterate (unable to read and write), and they relied on their priests to tell them what the Bible said. They were also superstitious, so they were willing to believe priests who said that natural disasters and the plague (see below) were punishments from God. During the Renaissance, Europe was primarily Catholic, and those who weren't (generally Jews and Muslims*) did their best to avoid attracting the Church's attention because it punished and persecuted those who were not Catholic.

> * People who believe in **Islam**, the second largest religion in the world after Christianity, are called Muslims. Islam emerged in the early seventh century.

Between 1095 and 1291, the Church led eight **crusades*** against the **Seljuk Turks** (an early Muslim empire) to wrest (take) control of the **Holy Land** (modern Israel) for Christians. The crusaders briefly gained control of the Holy Land, but the Muslims eventually drove them all out.

> * The Crusades were a series of eight "holy wars" in which Christian Europeans tried to drive the Muslims out of the Holy Land.

Divine Right of Kings: The divine right of kings was the belief that God personally chose the rulers for each country. Once people noticed that many of their "divinely appointed" kings didn't seem to care if their subjects were cold and hungry, they began wondering if their rulers had lied to them. They noticed that the clergy* supported the king's decisions most of the time and connected these observations to their complaints about corrupt priests. Increasingly, people viewed the government and the Church as united against everyone else.

> * Clergy: religious leaders. Other names common on the SAT for Christian religious leaders: *abbess, abbot, chaplain, cleric, confessor, curate, deacon, dean, divine, minister, monk, nun, parson, pastor,*

preacher, prelate, priest, pulpiteer, rector, shepherd and *vicar*.

Feudalism: The **feudal system** was a system in which land and protection were given to people in exchange for service. People were divided into **nobles** (landowners) and **serfs** (peasants). The nobles owned **manors**, which were like small, self-sufficient villages. The work of the manor—farming, raising livestock, grinding grain, and fermenting beer—was done by serfs, who were forbidden to leave the manor without their noble's permission. They paid rent to the noble in the form of goods and services. If the land was sold, the serfs were included in the new owner's property.

Chivalry: All knights were expected to follow the **chivalric code**, a system designed to ensure that they used their fighting skills to protect the weak, obey their king, and defend the Church against unbelievers. In return for service, serfs could expect their nobles to protect them from other nobles who might attack them or demand their property. However, many nobles did not honor their commitments to the chivalric code.

Ottoman Empire*: In 1299, the **Ottoman Empire** was formed by **Osman**, a Muslim Turkish leader. About fifty years later, the empire invaded western Europe, seeking land, power, and the conversion of Christians to Islam. Both Christians and Muslims saw members of the other's faith as infidels (unbelievers) and tried to kill or convert as many as possible. The Ottoman Empire was the stronger of the two for several centuries. At times, it controlled a large section of Europe as well as territory in Asia,

North Africa, and the Middle East. The Ottoman Empire ended in 1922, and as you will see, it participated in many events that are covered in this book.

> * An **empire** is a collection of smaller kingdoms, states, or territories that each have their own ruler. Each ruler answers to the **emperor** (highest monarch) and is responsible for paying tribute (taxes) and providing soldiers for the empire's armies.

Spanish Inquisition (1478–1834): The Catholic Church began the **Inquisition** (interrogation) to combat religious heresies (wrong beliefs) and prevent their spread. In practice, this meant targeting Jews and Muslims. In 1478, the Pope (head of the Catholic Church) authorized **Ferdinand and Isabella**, the Catholic monarchs of Spain, to begin the Spanish Inquisition and rid Spain of everyone who wasn't Catholic. In 1492*, the Spanish rulers defeated the last Muslim stronghold in Spain, making it an officially Catholic nation. They also exiled all Jews living in Spain, saying they could only stay if they converted to Christianity. Many Jews had already converted to Christianity at sword point, and many of these "new Christians" continued to practice Judaism in secret despite the torture and death they would suffer if caught.

> * 1492 is the same year that Christopher Columbus "discovered" the Americas, where millions of the people we now call Native Americans already lived.

Since forcible conversions don't change what people believe, the Spanish Inquisition spent the next hundred years persecuting the new converts for not being "really" Christian. In 1609, Spain expelled (deported) its entire remaining Muslim population, at least twice as many as had been targeted during Spain's expulsion of the Jews in 1492. The removal of Muslims was especially cruel because it consisted of forced marches under military guards who even made people pay for the privilege of drinking water from a stream on their way to the border.

Fear of the plague* also fanned the flames of the Spanish Inquisition. Anyone who seemed immune was suspected of being in league with dark forces bent on humanity's destruction.

* | The Bubonic Plague began in 1347.

Similar superstitions also led to many accusations of witchcraft throughout Europe, and these often led to torture and executions. Women were the main targets of witchcraft accusations, although some men were also accused.

Historians have connected the expulsions of the Jews and Muslims from Catholic Spain to the development of **race-based slavery**, a concept that designated (chose) which people could be enslaved and made to work without pay. Like Spain, the rest of Europe was prejudiced against non-Christians and **xenophobic** (disliking or fearing foreigners). Europeans were especially afraid that people who dressed and acted like good Christians were really secret Jews or secret Muslims. To allay (lessen) their fears, some European countries required Jews to wear special hats or clothing to indicate their alien (outsider) status and forced them to live in crowded ghettos* (walled-off city neighborhoods). In Spain, the Arabic language was outlawed and known Muslims had to keep their front doors open on Fridays, the weekly Islamic holy day, to prove they were not worshiping as Muslims.

> *　*Ghettos* are segregated neighborhoods for unpopular minority groups and the poor. The first ones, for Jews, were walled off, but today they are mostly not. Synonyms include *tenement, slum, the 'hood,* and *shanty town.*

These restrictions on non-Christians helped Europeans get comfortable with the idea that a person's skin color could also be a marker of second-class citizenship. At the same time, Christian Europeans and Americans realized that if they enslaved dark-skinned people, those people would have a hard time escaping and blending in with the general (white) population. In other words, European Christians had two belief systems—one based on religion and one based on race—that intertwined (combined) in their minds to convince them that they were better than everyone else. From there, it became easy to believe that God had appointed white Christians to rule over dark-skinned non-Christians because dark-skinned people were seen as deceitful (dishonest), demonic, and dirty.

The fall of the last Muslim fortress in Spain to the armies of Ferdinand and Isabella during the last Crusade meant that Muslims had been forced out of western Europe. Islam ceased to be an influence on European culture and instead became associated with "the East*." Europe became "the West" and almost exclusively Christian. Jews were alternately well-treated and scorned, depending on politics and the preferences of European rulers.

* The East is also divided into the "Orient," or Asia, and the "Levant," or Middle East. The West is also known as the "Occident."

United Kingdom: To understand the Middle Ages in the United Kingdom, you first need some background information that all student test-takers are generally expected to know and that can be referenced in SAT READING literature and history passages. The following section is an extremely skimpy version of the events in British history that influenced the development of the ideas of democracy on which the United States is founded. It omits (leaves out) centuries of fascinating wars, murder, royal intrigue, and empire building unless they connect directly to what you need to know for the SAT.

The **British Isles** are a collection of islands about thirty miles from the western coast of France in the northern Atlantic Ocean. The largest island is called **Great Britain** and it includes **England, Scotland,** and **Wales.** These countries and **Northern Ireland** comprise (make up) the **United Kingdom.**

The original inhabitants of Great Britain and **Ireland** were **Celts,** a collection of central European tribes who were driven from their land in Europe by the **Roman Empire** during the first century and settled on the British Isles.

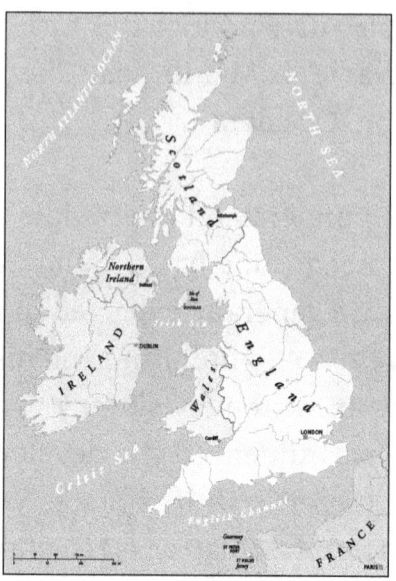

The British Isles include over six thousand islands.

The island of Great Britain was invaded by the Roman Empire in 43 CE*, during the reign of **Julius Caesar**. The Romans built roads, founded the town of Londinium (London), and imposed law and order. Their language—Latin—became the language of government, written communication, and business because the Celts lacked a common language and had not yet developed writing. In addition, many Roman soldiers, who came from all parts of the far-flung empire, chose to settle in Great Britain when they retired from military service. As a result, the British Isles became home to a diverse population.

    * Common Era (CE or C.E.): A secular (non-religious) way of referring to years in the Gregorian** Calendar, which uses the year of Jesus's birth as year one.

   ** Named for Pope Gregory XIII***.

✳✳✳

Roman Numeral 1 to 1000

I	V	X	L	C	D	M
1	5	10	50	100	500	1000

1	I	11	XI	200	CC
2	II	20	XX	300	CCC
3	III	30	XXX	400	CD
4	IV	40	XL	500	D
5	V	50	L	600	DC
6	VI	60	LX	700	DCC
7	VII	70	LXX	800	DCCC
8	VIII	80	LXXX	900	CM
9	IX	90	XC	1000	M
10	X	100	C	1001	MI

Roman numerals are frequently used in the titles of rulers and other leaders.

In 122 CE, the Romans built **Hadrian's Wall** on the border between England and Scotland to deter invaders. It was about eight feet wide, twelve feet high and seventy-three miles long. It stretched from coast to coast. Today, only about one-tenth of the wall remains. It is a major tourist attraction and was named a World Heritage Site* in 1987.

✳ | World Heritage Sites are named by the United Nations.

In the fifth century, the **Angles**, **Saxons**, and **Jutes** (Germanic tribes) invaded Great Britain. These new groups quickly gained political and cultural dominance. The name *England* comes from the word *Angles*. The Anglo-Saxon language is a version of early

German and one of the main root languages of modern English*. It contributes many one- and two-syllable words such as *axe, daughter, battle, brother, king, marsh, meadow, needle,* and *queen.*

> ✳ English vocabulary is 29 percent Latin, 29 percent French, and 26 percent Anglo-Saxon. About 6 percent comes from Greek.

England's conversion to Christianity began in the sixth century. The stories of **King Arthur and the Round Table** concern the efforts of Christian rulers to eradicate (destroy) the pagan religions of the region.

Vikings from Scandinavia* began raiding English coastal villages during the ninth century. In 877, **Alfred the Great**, a prince of the English kingdom of Wessex, led the English to victory over the Danish Viking army in the **Battle of Ashdown**. Later military victories allowed Alfred to enact the **Danelaw** which limited Viking territory in England and forced many Vikings to convert to Christianity.

> ✳ Denmark, Norway, and Sweden.

In 1066, Vikings led by **William, Duke of Normandy***, invaded because the English king had named him the heir to the throne. However, when the king died, a rival prince had himself crowned. William invaded, won a decisive victory against the English in the **Battle of Hastings** in 1066, became king, and became known as **William the Conqueror**.

> ✳ Normandy is in northern France.

In the twelfth century, King Richard I of England went on the **Third Crusade**, leaving his brother John to rule during his absence. Richard was captured and held hostage for an extremely high ransom by the **Duke of Austria**. When the ransom was paid, he returned to England as a hero and gained the nickname, **Richard the Lionheart**. However, he went to war against Phillip II of France almost immediately and died in battle about five years later. The **Robin Hood** stories—about a band of outlaws who steal from the rich to give to the poor—are set during Richard's absence and end with his triumphant return to England.

Unlike his brother Richard, King John I was an unpopular leader. He lost the French territory that had belonged to England since the days of William the Conqueror. When he tried to raise taxes to pay for his failed campaigns, civil war broke out. It ended when John agreed in June of 1215 to sign the **Magna Carta** (Great Charter), a document that has strong similarities to the **United States Declaration of Independence**, **Constitution** and **Bill of Rights**. It says that everyone—even the king—must obey the law. It also says that the ruler cannot raise taxes without the approval of his government, that people cannot be arrested or jailed for no reason, and that martial law cannot be imposed during peacetime.

The Renaissance (1300–1600)

The history that you most need to know for SAT begins in the fourteenth century, at the beginning of the Renaissance (the European cultural, social, artistic, and political "rebirth" that occurred after the Middle Ages).

Bubonic Plague, or Black Death, killed between 50 and 60 percent of Europe's population—about 25 million people—in fourteenth-century Europe. Some historians argue that this high mortality rate led people to doubt God and the teachings of the Church, setting the stage for the **Protestant Reformation** (see below) as well as for more generalized questioning of religious "truth." This questioning was helped along by the scientific discoveries of the Renaissance. People saw that science seemed to contradict long-held beliefs about the place of humanity in the universe. People began to question what they had been taught about God's word and God's will.

No one at that time understood how the Black Death was transmitted*. Since it was highly contagious, almost always fatal, and an absolutely awful way to die, people were desperate to understand why God would allow so much suffering. They were also easily persuaded that the plague was the work of Satan and his human minions (servants); this superstition often led to pogroms (organized attacks) and killings.

> * In the 1890s, French scientists determined that the bacteria that causes Bubonic plague was transmitted by fleas, whose bites transferred the disease from infected rats to people. This was convincing because at the time, most Europeans had fleas or flea bites because they generally didn't bathe, wear clean clothes, or sleep in clean bedding. However, scientists now think that the plague can also spread through air transmission. You could get an SAT READING science passage about this discovery or other significant breakthroughs in epidemiology (the study of how epidemics spread).

Asian Influences on Europe: In the 1400s, Europeans began to realize that the Ottoman Empire was more than just an economic and military threat and religious adversary (opponent). Although the Empire was officially Muslim, it welcomed people of all faiths and nationalities, and this tolerance helped it become a center of learning and innovation that surpassed anything that Christian Europe had to offer. Islamic scientists had revolutionized navigation (sailing) by inventing the compass and the astrolabe (a device that helped sail by the stars). Islamic mathematicians invented algebra. Islamic physicians, some of whom were women, invented music therapy, which they used to treat patients in hospitals, which themselves were another Ottoman Empire invention.

The Chinese also had inventions to offer—noodles, silk, and gunpowder—and Europeans were quick to realize that the sale of these new products throughout Asia and the Middle East could be quite profitable. Trade routes and commerce developed, and people traveled to new places, sometimes as slaves. New technologies were invented and shared. Diseases spread to new continents. European scholars "discovered" Greek and Roman texts that had been preserved by the Ottomans but largely forgotten in Europe for centuries.

All this interaction with foreign lands was exciting. Renaissance philosophers* began to rethink much of what they had always believed to be true about God and humanity's place in the universe, a process that resulted in **humanism**, the belief that people can solve their own problems by using their **reason**.

> * A philosopher studies philosophy, which is the study of the meaning of life, the universe, and human existence. Philosophers are also concerned with finding the best way for people to live. The word "philosophy" literally means "one who loves knowledge" because "*philo*" means "one who loves" and "*soph*" means "wisdom."

Reason: Humanists believe that people can understand the world and shape it to suit their needs by observing and thinking. Whenever you see the term "reason" on SAT READING, you should understand it as the belief that the human mind can figure out pretty much everything without reference to religious doctrine* or God. Renaissance philosophers believed that science was the surest way to learn how God wanted people to behave. Humanist ideas formed the core beliefs of the Renaissance and led directly to the ideas of American democracy, as will become clear.

> * Doctrine: a set of beliefs promoted by a political party, religious authority, or other group. Synonyms include *dogma, tenet, creed,* and *credo.*

Niccolò Machiavelli: Often cited as the inventor of political science*, Machiavelli wrote *The Prince*, a reason-based work that has been excerpted for SAT READING passages. It argues that a good ruler knows that his subjects are motivated by their own self-interests but that he must be prepared to act unscrupulously (immorally) when necessary for the good of the state. In fact, his argument in defense of such behavior is so famous that the adjective "Machiavellian" is used as a synonym for cunning (trickery) and cruelty. His work is still read and taught in colleges today, and you can assume that his status as the inventor of political science means that all the writers who wrote about government and politics between Machiavelli's lifetime and ours have read *The Prince* as part of their own education. In other words, "all well-educated people" know who Machiavelli is, so you should, too.

> * Political science is the study of government systems, behavior, and activity.

Renaissance Women: Although most women's lives centered around their homes and families at this time, there were some important exceptions. **Christine de Pisan**, who lived in the court of King Charles V of France, wrote strongly in defense of women's rights. **Eleanor of Aquitaine**, who was both a queen and the mother of several kings*, corresponded (exchanged letters) with kings and popes about political and religious matters. The writing of either woman could be selected as an SAT READING passage, as could a letter or essay by **Queen Elizabeth I** of England. In general, any passage by a Renaissance woman writer is likely to be about limitations on women's lives and the injustices they suffered under male rule. This is also true of women writers from later historical periods.

> * Including King Richard I (the Lionheart) and King John I who signed the Magna Carta.

Renaissance Inventions:
- **Movable Type and the Printing Press:** In 1440, **Johannes Gutenberg** invented a printing press with movable type, pre-carved letters that could be moved around to form words as needed. This was a big improvement over writing everything by hand or carving a new set of type on blocks of wood for

every text. Bibles and other texts could now be reproduced much more quickly and cheaply than ever before, and this increased people's interest in learning to read. Perhaps most importantly, people were now able to read the Bible. Instead of having to simply believe what their priests told them, people could now read it for themselves.

- **Glass Lenses:** People discovered how to grind, shape, and polish glass to improve human vision, and this led to the invention of eyeglasses, microscopes, and telescopes.

- **Microscope:** Probably first invented in the 1590s, microscopes allowed people to see parts of the physical world that they had never known existed, such as red blood cells, bacteria, and yeast and protozoa (single-celled organisms). These discoveries radically changed how Europeans understood the physical universe and eventually led to huge advances in medical treatments.

- **Telescope:** Improvements in glass lens technology led to the invention of telescopes, which allowed astronomers such as Galileo and Copernicus to observe the night sky in more detail than ever before. Their discoveries challenged the belief that Earth was the center of the universe and suggested that the Church's teaching that the sun revolved around the Earth was wrong.

Renaissance Music: The printing press made sheet music possible. This led to a written system of musical notation so that musicians could understand how to play individual songs without having to hear them first. **Polyphonic music** (the combination of several musical melodies at once) was invented, and this led to the development of madrigals* and opera. The harpsichord and church organ were also invented. Articles about the development of different kinds of musical styles and instruments have appeared on SAT WRITING.

    * | A song for four to six people singing *a capella* (without instrumental accompaniment).

Renaissance Art: Rulers, wealthy aristocrats, and Church officials supported artists in a patronage system in which artists received financial support in exchange for doing their art. New paints and painting techniques were developed. Three-dimensional painting (painting that uses perspective to represent depth or distance on a two-dimensional surface) was developed. Both SAT READING and SAT WRITING can include essays about art, and many of these assume that the reader has a basic understanding of European art history. You should know that **Leonardo da Vinci** and **Michelangelo** are the two most important Italian Renaissance artists. Two others are **Raphael** and **Donatello**; fans of *Teenage Mutant Ninja Turtles* will recognize these names. There's also **Botticelli**, but he isn't a Ninja Turtle.

Da Vinci is known for his "science fiction" ideas—submarines, helicopters, and other inventions—as well as for his pop culture status as a cultural icon (symbol), as in Dan Brown's novel, *The Da Vinci Code*. Da Vinci's two most famous paintings are *Mona Lisa* and *The Last Supper*. *Mona Lisa* is the most famous painting in the world, and just about everybody on earth knows what it looks like. Multiple SAT WRITING passages discuss it and its fame. *The Last Supper* portrays a critical moment in the life of Jesus Christ as it is described in the Christian Bible.

Passages about Leonardo da Vinci's innovative painting technique have appeared on **SAT WRITING**.

Da Vinci's use of symbolism in *The Last Supper* has been debated for centuries.

Michelangelo's work is similarly important. He created the beautiful paintings on the ceiling of the Sistine Chapel in Rome and the marble statue of David. The authors of the material selected for the test will also assume that you know what these works of art look like.

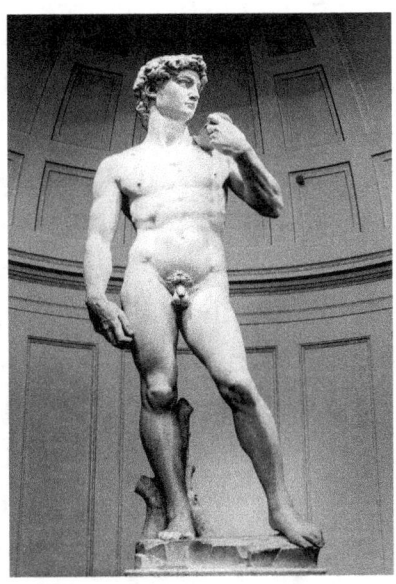

Michelangelo's 1504 depiction of the Biblical character David focuses on the moments before his decisive battle with the giant Goliath.

Michelangelo painted the Sistine Chapel ceiling with scenes from the Bible between 1508 and 1512.

Protestant Reformation: The Protestant Reformation is generally not included on the SAT directly because it was a religious conflict that took place in Europe before the United States was a country. However, knowing about it helps to explain why some groups left Europe and traveled to the Americas in search of religious freedom.

The people who started the Protestant (from the word "protest") Reformation were protesting the Catholic Church, which they accused of corruption, hypocrisy (saying one thing and doing another), and tyranny (dictatorship) over the people. Although the majority of Catholic priests honored their oaths of chastity (no sex) and poverty and did their best to help people, a significant number of higher-level clergy had children with their mistresses (women they were not married to). The sale of indulgences (pieces of paper to help the bearer get into Heaven) that granted absolution (forgiveness for sins) to sinners also enriched members of the clergy and was seen as problematic because it meant the rich had an easier path to Heaven than the poor.

Martin Luther began the Protestant Reformation in 1517 by nailing his **"Ninety-Five Theses"** (ninety-five proposals condemning the excesses and corruption of the Catholic Church) to the door of his local church. He hoped to start a public debate about the sale of indulgences and argued that God forgives only those who have faith. The document, written in the scholar's language of Latin, which most people couldn't understand, was taken from the door of his church and copies were made in German. In response, the Catholic Church excommunicated (expelled) Martin Luther from religious worship, declared him an outlaw, and granted permission for anyone to kill him. He was, however, protected by Prince Frederick III of the German state of Saxony. Luther spent the next ten years translating the Bible from Latin to German. Many of the European groups who settled North America were Protestants, and their religious views influenced the laws by which the new colonies were governed. Until Luther, "Catholic" and "Christian" basically meant the same thing in Europe. During the Protestant Reformation, however, many people broke away from the Catholic Church, and since they didn't all agree with each other, many new sects (groups with different beliefs) formed. In other words, one result of the Protestant Reformation was that there were now many different kinds of Christians, including Lutheran, Calvinist*, Methodist, Presbyterian, Quaker**, and Baptist.

> *   Followers of John Calvin, who broke away from the Catholic Church in about 1530.

> **   Quakers played an important role in the efforts to end American slavery.

Many of the early Pilgrims (people on a religious quest) who sailed to North America in search of religious freedom were **Calvinists**, and their thinking influenced American political thought. For example, **President Ronald Reagan** borrowed the Calvinist idea of America as a "shining city on a hill" that would lead the rest of the world into peace and prosperity. Reagan used the phrase in his final speech as president to describe the United States as a beacon of light in a world threatened by nuclear war and the Soviet Union. It's possible that Reagan's speech could be selected for SAT READING.

Luther and other Protestant leaders translated the Latin Bible that the Catholic Church used into everyday German, French, and English so that even those who hadn't learned Latin could read it. Once people could read the Bible for themselves, they had questions about differences between what they read and what their priests said. The Church authorities did not like to be questioned and used tactics from the Inquisition (such as torture and public executions) to keep troublemakers in line. These tactics sparked almost 150 years of religious war in Europe and prompted Protestant groups like the Pilgrims to evade persecution by sailing to North America.

These religious wars between Catholic rulers and Protestant rulers swept across Europe (including England and Scotland) from 1517 to 1648 and affected European politics and thought in numerous ways. In England, **King Henry VIII** left the Catholic Church when the Pope denied his request to annul (cancel) his marriage to **Catherine of Aragon** because she had not produced a son. He established the **Church of England**, which permitted divorce, and he went on to have five more wives* in his quest for a male heir to the throne. He also made the Church of England the official state religion. He outlawed Catholicism, plundered (robbed) Catholic monasteries, and confiscated their lands. Many Catholics and suspected Catholics were arrested, tortured, and executed. After Henry's death, **Mary**, his daughter by his first wife, Catherine of Aragon, became queen and switched the country back to Catholicism. When she died, her Protestant half sister **Elizabeth** became queen and outlawed Catholicism once again.

> * King Henry VIII's other five wives were Anne Boleyn, Jane Seymour, Anne of Cleves, Catherine Howard, and Katherine Parr.

Other countries also switched from Catholic to Protestant and back again with each new leader. As a result of all these political and religious flip-flops, trust in religion weakened and many people turned to new paradigms (a set of assumptions or ideas; a prototype or archetype) that prioritized the observations of human beings over blind faith and superstition. Although most Europeans still believed in God, they were increasingly likely to agree with the humanist belief that human intelligence could solve most problems.

Age of Exploration: In 1453, the Ottoman Empire captured the city of Constantinople (Istanbul), removing the last major stronghold of Christianity in eastern Europe and blocking traditional routes between Europe and Asia.

Renamed Istanbul in 1453, Constantinople served as a gateway between eastern Europe and Turkey.

In response, Portuguese explorers searched for other routes, such as sailing around the southern tip of Africa into the Indian Ocean. One of these explorers, **Christopher Columbus**, believed he could sail from Europe to China by sailing across the Atlantic Ocean. He made four trips looking for this route to Asia but landed in the Americas instead.

Portugal and Spain built their world empires in the Americas, Asia, and Africa during the fifteenth and sixteenth centuries (the 1400s–1500s). At first, Portugal controlled Brazil, Venezuela, and Uruguay, but it later gave Venezuela and Uruguay to Spain. In the first act of European empire-building, the Portuguese and Spanish divided this "New World" of non-Christian nations populated by dark-skinned "savages" between them so that they could exploit its resources without antagonizing (angering) each other.

Race-Based Slavery: Slavery has existed for as long as human societies have existed. Historically, enslavement could happen to anyone. People became slaves for many reasons, including when they were conquered in war, when they did not practice the right religion, or when they were too poor to support themselves or pay their debts. They could earn their freedom, and if they did, their children would not be born enslaved. However, the Europeans who colonized the Americas redefined slavery to include two groups of dark-skinned peoples: Native Americans and Africans.

When Columbus landed in the Americas, he viewed the people living there as potential slaves and saw their land and possessions as riches for his employers, Ferdinand and Isabella of Spain. The Spanish established settlements in South and Central America, where they destroyed the Aztec, Mayan, and Incan empires, conquered Mexico and many Caribbean islands, and even claimed the entire Pacific Ocean for Spain. Passages about the destruction of the empires and the **Taino** people (indigenous inhabitants of what are now Cuba, Jamaica, Haiti, the Dominican Republic, Puerto Rico, and the Virgin Islands) have appeared on SAT WRITING.

Like the Spanish, the Englishmen who colonized the Americas believed that they were racially and morally superior to the darker-skinned, non-Christian peoples they encountered, and they enslaved as many as five million of them beginning in 1492. **John Smith**, the leader of England's first successful colony, the **Jamestown Settlement*** in Virginia, agreed with the Spanish that the Native Americans tribe they encountered were suitable only for "drudgery, work, and slavery" even though his entire colony relied on trade with them for food. By 1610, violence had broken out between the settlement and the surrounding tribes, and the English had begun enslaving native prisoners of war.

✳ | Jamestown was settled in 1607.

Pilgrims: In 1608, a group of English Calvinists fled England to avoid persecution by the Church of England. They lived in Holland for about a decade before deciding that relocating to an English colony offered them the best chance at having both religious freedom and economic prosperity. They embarked (set sail) for Virginia on the *Mayflower*, but storms and poor navigation led them hundreds of miles off course to Massachusetts. Faced with low supplies and the coming of winter, they decided to settle wherever they could land. While still on board the *Mayflower*, they wrote the **Mayflower Compact**, a short document that said the signatories (signers) agreed to unite and form a government that would govern their colony. The authority for this government would come from the people themselves rather than from a king. Although the compact was an informal document, it is regarded as an important early example of democratic government.

Like the Jamestown settlers, the Pilgrims had few scruples (little hesitation) about exploiting the area and its inhabitants, the **Wampanoag**. When outbreaks of European diseases* killed many Wampanoag, the Pilgrims thanked God for allowing them to claim Wampanoag land, which they cleared of trees to make space for tobacco plantations.

* | Historians estimate that between 90 and 95 percent
   | of the native population of the Americas died
   | from European diseases from which they
   | had no immunity.

When the English settled in Massachusetts, they upset the existing power balance between Dutch settlers and the **Pequot**, the most powerful tribe in the region. During the **Pequot War** (1636–1638), the **Narragansett** and **Mohegan** tribes sided with the English because they were enemies of the Pequot. Atrocities occurred on both sides, but the war is most famous for the **Battle of Mistick Fort**, during which the English and their allies burned a Pequot village. Hundreds burned to death or were shot trying to escape the flames. In the days that followed, hundreds more Pequot were captured. The men were shot, and the women and children were enslaved. Some were given to the Narragansett and Mohegan tribes in gratitude for their alliance with the British, and some were enslaved on local English farms. However, the majority were exported to the Caribbean, which ensured that they could never escape or return home. By the 1660s, thousands of Native Americans had been enslaved. Some tribes kidnapped members of other tribes for sale into slavery. Some historians believe that these tribes may have done so to prevent the Europeans from trying to enslave them. By the time they realized that the Europeans would not honor their agreements, tribal society had lost so many people from disease, war, and enslavement that they were powerless to stop further encroachments (intrusions) on their land, livelihoods, and freedom.

Enslaved Africans probably arrived in the Americas with the first European explorers in the late 1400s. Christopher Columbus sailed on Portuguese slave ships before he sailed to the Americas, and his diaries show his interest in enslaving Native Americans as well. Early European explorers and settlers used a mixture of poor white people, indentured* Europeans, enslaved Africans, Native Americans, and convicts to supply the labor force for the **colonies****. Since plantation owners wanted to make a profit, they were attracted to the idea of an enslaved workforce because such workers did not have to be paid or even treated very well. (Enslaved people were provided with food, clothing, and shelter, but usually just enough so they could work.) Although white Europeans were generally uncomfortable with enslaving other white Christians, they were less concerned with the morality of enslaving people from other races or religions.

* People who signed contracts agreeing to perform unpaid labor for a certain amount of time, often to cover the cost of crossing the Atlantic Ocean by ship.

** **Colonies** are governed by an occupying empire or nation. A colony's primary purpose is to be a resource for its parent state. Examples of early colonies include the Virginia Colony, the New York Colony, and the Massachusetts Colony. The Plymouth Colony, settled by the Pilgrims, is not considered one of the thirteen colonies in America because it was disestablished in 1691.

By 1526, almost a century before the 1619 arrival of enslaved Africans in Jamestown, Virginia, there were African slaves in a Spanish colony in South Carolina, and they later accompanied the Spanish when they expanded into Florida. The British explorer **Sir Francis Drake** may also have brought enslaved Africans to **Roanoke, Virginia**; he and a cousin "owned" over twelve hundred enslaved Africans.

The idea of using race to mark Africans for enslavement was encouraged by the Christian European belief that dark skin was God's way of identifying which people they were allowed to enslave. African rulers, accustomed to enslaving their enemies, were happy to sell people into European slavery in exchange for guns, mirrors, and other goods that were unavailable in Africa. In what came to be known as the "Triangle Trade," European ships brought goods to African leaders in exchange for prisoners who had been captured in Africa's interior. These newly enslaved people were then transported to the Americas on overcrowded ships. This forced voyage of enslaved Africans is known as the **Middle Passage**. Once in the Americas, this human cargo was sold to plantation owners. The ships then sailed home to Europe with their riches—cotton, tobacco, and sugar—to buy more European merchandise to exchange for new African slaves.

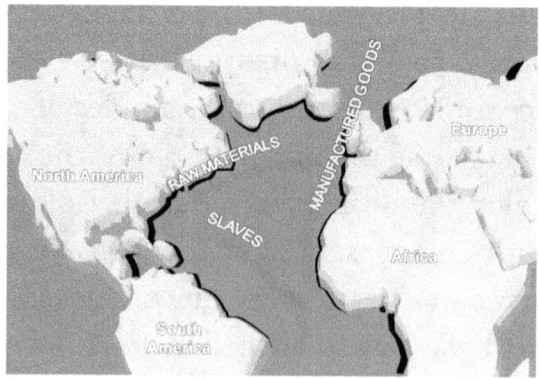

How the Triangle Trade moved people and goods.

European and American uses of racial stereotyping, enslavement, and violence were not really taught in American K-12 schools until about twenty-five years ago, when the United States began to reevaluate the long-term effects of racial inequality and injustice. SAT READING passages that address racially motivated violence are becoming more frequent as the United States grapples with how it has historically used the slave labor of racial minorities to enrich white people. An increasing number of SAT READING passages—including those used for the literature passages—are written from perspectives of minority groups and can be from any time in American history.

The Enlightenment (1685–1815)

The Enlightenment was a European intellectual movement of the seventeenth and eighteenth centuries that emphasized reason and individualism rather than tradition. It is known as the "long century" because it covered a period of 130 years. In fact, it's hard to know for certain when the Renaissance ends and the Enlightenment begins. Generally, the Enlightenment covers the eighteenth century (1700s), which saw the Industrial Revolution, the American Revolution, and the French Revolution. This is not a coincidence. Enlightenment ideas are humanist ideas (see previous section). Most Europeans believed in the primacy (superiority) of reason over superstition and ignorance. Increasing knowledge about the physical world—thanks to Renaissance inventions like microscopes and telescopes—also led people to question religious beliefs and the divine right of kings. Other Renaissance ideas, such as race-based slavery, continue to affect the lives of people living today, both in the United States and worldwide. As a result, these ideas turn up on SAT READING.

Enlightenment thinkers believed that humanity could use reason to learn everything and solve the great questions of just about every topic. In France, **Denis Diderot** created an encyclopedia (the *Encyclopédie*) to hold all of human knowledge. One of his contemporaries (people alive during his lifetime) called him "the first great writer who belonged wholly and undividedly to modern democratic society." Passages about Diderot's *Encyclopédie* could appear on SAT WRITING.

Social Contract: A social contract is a real or theoretical (in theory) agreement between rulers and the people they rule. It includes the rights and responsibilities of both the ruler and the ruled. Several Enlightenment philosophers developed their own theories of the social contract, and their ideas had a direct impact on the birth of the United States.

Glorious Revolution: In 1688, a three-year political struggle over the English throne ended without violence, giving it two names: the **Glorious Revolution** and the **Bloodless Revolution**. It began in 1685, when **King James II** was crowned King of England. England was an officially Protestant nation and an absolute monarchy (a country in which the king or queen has complete power over everything). However, James had converted to Catholicism years before becoming king at fifty-one years old. When he was crowned, he angered many of the British nobility by being too friendly to France and reversing some anti-Catholic laws. His daughter, **Mary**, however, had been raised Protestant. In 1677, she married the Protestant **Prince William of Orange** of the Netherlands.

In 1688, James II's second wife gave birth to a baby boy, and James announced that this child, who would inherit the English throne, would be raised as a Catholic. In response, a group of

English nobles invited William of Orange to invade England and take the throne from James, his father-in-law.

As it happened, William was already planning to invade England, and he attacked with a large army. Many of James's Protestant troops defected (switched sides), and James eventually escaped to France, where King Louis XIV allowed him to stay until his death.

England suddenly found itself without a monarch. The British Parliament (the governing body of England) averted (prevented) war by agreeing that William and Mary could rule jointly, but only if they agreed to sign the **English Bill of Rights**, a document that expressed many Enlightenment ideals. For example, it rejected the divine right of kings and decreed that the king needed Parliament's approval to go to war or raise taxes. It also guaranteed that ordinary citizens had the right to bear arms in self-defense and prohibited excessive bail and cruel and unusual punishment. The English Bill of Rights is generally regarded as an important influence on the United States' Bill of Rights, which was written about a century later.

Enlightenment Thinkers: Thomas Hobbes was an English philosopher who believed that the natural state of humanity was war and chaos. In 1651, he published *Leviathan**, which argues that only a strong, authoritarian leader can provide the stability necessary for a society to flourish. He described life without such a leader as "solitary, poor, nasty, brutish and short," and is famous for his negative opinion of human nature. Hobbes's ideas influenced many later Enlightenment philosophers, and passages taken from his work have appeared on SAT READING.

* In the Bible, leviathan means "sea monster." Hobbes used the term as a metaphor for a strong, powerful society.

Another English philosopher, **John Locke**, disagreed with Hobbes. He said that a newborn baby is a *tabula rasa* (blank slate) and that the goal of education was to teach children moral behavior. In 1689, Locke published *Two Treatises of Government* in which he challenged the divine right of kings to rule, arguing instead that a ruler's power comes from the consent and will of the people. He also said each person is born with "natural rights" to "life, liberty, and the pursuit of property," a phrase that **Thomas Jefferson** later modified to read, "life, liberty, and the pursuit of happiness" in the **Declaration of Independence** (see below). Passages from Locke's work have also appeared on SAT READING.

Work by the Swiss philosopher **Jean-Jacques Rousseau** has also been on SAT READING. Like Locke, Rousseau believed that people were innately good at birth. In 1762, he published *The Social Contract*, a book that begins with the dramatic line, "Man is born free and everywhere he is in chains." In it, Rousseau argues that human beings will only know true freedom when they live in a society whose government protects their rights.

All the Enlightenment philosophers agreed that every person is born with human rights that can never be taken away. Once this idea of "unalienable rights" (as Thomas Jefferson wrote it in the Declaration of Independence) took hold, it slowly began to undermine (weaken) the claims of people in authority that society was organized according to God's will. Over the next two centuries, challenges to race, gender, and income inequality became more common and more urgent. An expanding concept of human rights led eventually to the abolition (end) of race-based slavery as well as to the development of the civil rights movement for African Americans, the women's rights movement, and movements to claim equal rights for groups including Native Americans, Mexican Americans, immigrants, senior citizens, disabled Americans and those who are LGBTQ+*. It also led to the labor movement and the abolition of child labor. Speeches by important leaders who argue that these universal human rights should be applied to all Americans or all people are common on SAT READING.

* | LGBTQ+ stands for lesbian, gay, bisexual, transgender, and queer or questioning**.

** | Questioning one's sexual orientation or gender identity.

The American Revolution (1765–1783)

The seeds of the American Revolution were planted and spread by Enlightenment thinkers, and their influence lasted much longer than the Revolutionary War itself. Below is a select chronology (timeline) of some of the most important events and battles of the Revolution. Basically, you should know the main ideas, events, and battles of the Revolution so that you understand references that writers may make to them.

French and Indian War (1756–1763): Both the **French and Indian War** and French support of the American Revolutionary War were motivated by French hatred of the British. Also known as the **Seven Years War**, this struggle was primarily between the British, who had a skinny sliver of thirteen North American colonies on the east coast of North America, and the French, who controlled parts of Canada and everything west of the Appalachian Mountains. It was a complicated, multiparty war that involved forces from every European empire as well as from a number of Native American tribes. The British won and gained control over Canada and the Ohio River Valley (everything east of the Mississippi River). They also won Florida from the Spanish.

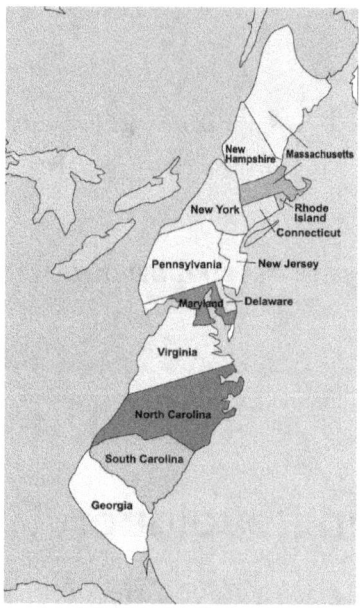

The thirteen colonies.

George Washington commanded British forces as a young man during the French and Indian War (although he led his men to defeat), and his experience gave him insight into how the British fought, which he later used as commander of the **American Continental Army** (an army of the thirteen colonies) during the American War of Independence. However, the American colonists who fought as British subjects in the war were angry at how little support the British provided them. They became even angrier when the English "rewarded" their sacrifice by requisitioning (demanding) their supplies and ammunition, conscripting (forcing) men to fight, and forcing colonists to accept British soldiers living in their homes, a practice that was so hated that it was later forbidden by the Third Amendment to the United States Constitution. The colonists' dissatisfaction only increased after the British raised taxes to pay for the French and Indian War and can be seen as a direct cause of the American Revolutionary War.

Tensions Rise in the American Colonies: The British Empire wanted its American colonies to be profitable to England, so they established a **mercantile** system in which colonists were only allowed to trade with the British, who also taxed British products that were imported to the colonies. The **Sugar Act** of 1764 and the **Stamp Act** of 1765 outraged the colonists, who saw them as "taxation without representation." Unlike British citizens in England, the colonists had no elected representatives in the British parliament but were still expected to pay taxes. Both Acts were so unpopular that the British repealed them in 1766. However, the **Townshend Acts** of 1767 were more inflammatory (offensive) because they:

- Imposed new taxes on glass, paper, lead, paint, and tea.
- Established a special military court to prosecute smugglers without a jury, thereby violating the five hundred-year-old right of every British citizen to a jury of their peers (equals, other citizens). The colonists, who still identified as British, saw this as a move to deprive them of full citizenship.
- Permitted British soldiers to search colonists' homes and businesses without a warrant. The American founders took this violation of privacy so seriously that they forbade it in the **Fourth Amendment** of the United States Constitution in 1789.

The Boston Massacre (March 5, 1770): In British-occupied Boston, an angry mob of colonists attacked on-duty British soldiers with sticks. The British fired on the crowd, killing five colonists and wounding six more. Among the dead was **Crispus Attucks,** who is believed to have been a native-born enslaved man who escaped to freedom and prospered as a sailor and rope maker. The British soldiers were put on trial in Boston, and future United States President **John Adams** defended them because of his strong belief in every person's right to a fair trial.

Boston Tea Party (December 16, 1773): The Boston Tea Party was the first overt (open) act of defiance against the British. Colonists dumped a large, very expensive cargo of tea that belonged to the British East India Company into Boston Harbor. The colonists wanted to protest yet another tax that they saw as unfair "taxation without representation."

The British responded to the Boston Tea Party by passing the **Intolerable Acts,** so called because the colonists saw them as too unjust to be tolerated (accepted). The Acts closed Boston Harbor until the colonists paid for the tea they had destroyed, revoked (took back) Massachusetts's historic right of self-governance, and required some colonists to travel to England for trial. This consequence (traveling to England for trial) imposed hardship on the accused because many of them could afford neither the time nor the expense of traveling to England. As a result, people accused of crimes had to forgo (give up) their right to a speedy trial as well as their right to a jury of their peers because their "peers" would be home in the colonies and unable to serve on a jury for a trial in England. The colonists believed so strongly in the right to a speedy trial by one's peers that it was added to the American Constitution as the **Sixth Amendment** in 1791.

First Continental Congress (September 5, 1774): Twelve colonies sent delegates to Philadelphia to organize the colonists' response to the Intolerable Acts. Only Georgia abstained. The colonists petitioned the English king, George III, for a fair hearing of their grievances, but this was denied.

Abigail Adams was the wife of **John Adams**, the United States' second president*. He participated in the Continental Congress in Philadelphia while she remained at home with their children in Massachusetts. Their correspondence (letters) has been used for paired passages on SAT READING. In one letter, Abigail tells her husband to "remember the ladies" and protect their rights as he and the other delegates designed the new United States government.

* Their son, John Quincy Adams, served as America's sixth president.

Patrick Henry: A vocal and passionate critic of the British king's efforts to subdue the American colonies, Henry distinguished himself by saying that he identified not as a Virginian but as an American. His 1775 speech, in which he says, "Give me liberty or give me death," is an impassioned defense of the American cause and has appeared on SAT READING.

Paul Revere's Ride: On the night of April 18, 1775, Paul Revere rode from Boston to Lexington, Massachusetts, (about 12.5 miles) to warn that British troops were approaching Lexington. This horseback ride was memorialized in 1860 by the American poet Henry Wadsworth Longfellow. Revere's timely (well-timed) warning contributed to American victories at the Battles of Lexington and Concord in Massachusetts.

Second Continental Congress (May 10, 1775): The delegates appointed generals for the Continental Army, approved the Declaration of Independence, and issued paper currency (money). They also wrote the **Articles of Confederation**, which established a new United States government. The Articles protected the independence of each state while also making it possible for them to work together as one nation for the purposes of international relations. However, the Articles gave too much power to the states and crippled the federal government's ability to act decisively or raise money to pay soldiers or its foreign debts.

Battle of Bunker Hill (June 17, 1775): This battle took place during the American siege (when a city or other location is completely surrounded by enemy forces) of British-held Boston. The British drove the Americans off the hill but suffered so many casualties that the Americans still felt that they had won.

Declaration of Independence (July 4, 1776): This document was written by Thomas Jefferson and adopted by the Second Continental Congress on July 4, 1776. Its preamble (introduction) has been used for SAT READING. It explains that the purpose of the new American government is to establish the rule of law, ensure peace domestically (inside the country), defend the country against its enemies, and protect the religious and political rights of its people. It lists the colonists' grievances against the English king, George III, and expresses the Enlightenment beliefs in universal human rights and a social contract between people and their government, and it is often quoted or alluded (referred) to in the constitutions of many democratic governments that modeled themselves on that of the United States. I have reproduced one of the more difficult parts and defined the words that my students tend not to know.

Prudence (caution), indeed, will dictate (say) that Governments long established should not be changed for light and transient (temporary) causes; and accordingly, all experience hath shewn (has shown), that mankind are more disposed to suffer, while evils are sufferable (tolerable), than to right themselves by abolishing (getting rid of) the forms to which they are accustomed. But when a long train (sequence) of abuses and usurpations (violations), pursuing invariably the same Object evinces (shows) a design (plan) to reduce them under absolute Despotism (tyranny, dictatorship), it is their right, it is their duty, to throw off such Government, and to provide new Guards for their future security.

In other words, the passage is saying that although you don't want to go around changing the government for a silly reason, when government becomes tyrannical (led by a tyrant or dictator), people have the right to get rid of the old government and select a new one that will work to make their lives better.

Thomas Paine (an English-born political philosopher and writer) published *Common Sense* in 1776, a pamphlet in which he argues for American independence from Britain. He advocated (supported) a democratic system in which elected delegates represent the people who elected them and protect their interests. Excerpts from *Common Sense* have appeared on SAT READING.

Washington Crosses the Delaware: In 1776, George Washington led 2,400 soldiers to a surprise Christmas Day attack on the British-led Hessian (German) forces that occupied Trenton, New Jersey. The Hessians, who assumed that there would not be an attack on the holiday, had celebrated Christmas Eve by getting drunk, so they were completely unprepared when the attack began. Over one thousand Hessians were captured, and only four American lives were lost.

Washington Crosses the Delaware, a famous
painting by Emanuel Leutze.

Battle of Saratoga (October 1777): This battle was actually three battles in three different places: Quebec, Canada; a farm in Saratoga, New York; and the Battle of Bemis Heights overlooking the Hudson River in New York. After terrible weather prevented a British retreat, they surrendered to the Continental Army. The Battle of Saratoga also set the stage for **Benedict Arnold's** eventual betrayal of the Americans*. In 1780, he conspired (plotted) with the British to surrender the military fort at West Point, New York. The plot failed, his partner was hanged, and Arnold escaped to the British.

>   * Arnold was angry because Washington didn't promote him despite his significant contributions to the Continental Army's victory at Saratoga.

Winter at Valley Forge (December 1777–June 1778): General Washington led his troops to Valley Forge, Pennsylvania, after losing two battles to the British. Despite extreme cold, hunger, and disease, the six-month break in the fighting allowed Washington to transform his troops from a ragtag (disorganized) group of farmers into a well-trained fighting force.

American Allies: In February of 1778, France* and Spain officially declared themselves as American allies. The French liked anyone who was fighting the British and had already been helping the Revolutionaries covertly (secretly) for over a year. Spain was interested in gaining more territory, which they did in west Florida. The entrance of these two world powers into the war drastically changed the balance of power and was essential to the eventual American victory.

> * The French nobleman, the **Marquis de Lafayette,** strongly supported the Revolution and assisted the Continental Army in battles in Pennsylvania. In the United States, he is generally regarded as an example of positive French-American relations.

Following their defeat by the Continental Army in Saratoga, the British concentrated their forces in their Southern colonies, where American **General Nathanael Greene** engaged them in what was primarily a guerrilla war*. The British suffered much higher casualties than the American forces did.

> * Guerrilla warfare: When small groups of unconventional combatants use ambushes, sabotage, and other targeted strikes against a larger traditional force.

Battle of Yorktown (September–October 1781): In the last land battle of the Revolution, American forces and their French allies besieged (put under siege) British-held Yorktown, Virginia. The British surrender was a major morale booster for the Americans, who then focused on driving the British out of the Southern colonies.

Treaty of Paris* (September 1783): This treaty ended the war and formalized America's independence. The new country now controlled all land east of the Mississippi River.

> * Treaties are often named after the location where they were signed.

Constitutional Convention (1787): After the war ended, delegates from every state except Rhode Island met in Philadelphia to revise the Articles of Confederation, which had created a weak federal government. For one hundred days, the delegates debated and wrote the **United States Constitution**, the document that lays out the framework of the federal government and the basic laws that govern all Americans. The process of writing it included heated debates about the structure of the federal government, the rights and responsibilities of the states, taxation, voting, and slavery. It was the world's first written constitution, and it has inspired the constitutions of over 150 countries.

Three-Fifths Compromise: Slavery was one of the most difficult issues facing the delegates at the convention. **The Three-Fifths Compromise** was intended to provide a political balance between states that permitted slavery and those that did not. Enslaved people were denied the right to "life, liberty, and the pursuit of happiness" that the Declaration of Independence said were the guaranteed rights of all people. On a practical level, however, many delegates were also enslavers whose economic well-being depended on the unpaid labor of slaves, and they were not willing to endorse (approve of) any language that sounded as if it might lead to abolishing slavery.

Slavery also complicated political representation and taxation. Georgia, the whitest Southern state, was only 62 percent white, whereas the Northern states were all at least 90 percent white. If only white people were counted in the census, the Northern states would have more representatives in Congress. They would also pay more taxes to the new federal government. However, if enslaved people were counted, the Southern states would pay more taxes and have more representatives. Eventually, the delegates agreed to count each enslaved person as three-fifths of a person so that the thirteen states would each have a fair share of Congressional delegates and tax responsibility.

United States Constitution: In 1788, the **United States Constitution** replaced the **Articles of Confederation** (see **Continental Congress** entry above). It established the structure of the federal government, how it would provide and pay for an army and navy, and how it would raise money to pay the nation's debts. It lists requirements that candidates for government positions must meet and specifies (spells out) what to do when government officials misbehave. Lastly, it details the process for adding amendments (additions) to the Constitution.

The **Bill of Rights** consists of the first ten amendments to the Constitution. It was ratified (approved) in 1791 and added to the Constitution to protect citizens from abuse by the federal government. Selections from the Bill of Rights have appeared as SAT READING passages, so here are the highlights. It is important to keep in mind that the second, third, and fourth amendments were based on the colonists' negative pre-Revolutionary War experiences with British soldiers.

The **First Amendment** guarantees freedom of religion, freedom of the press, the right to assemble (gather together) peaccably, and the right to protest government injustice.

The **Second Amendment** grants the right to bear arms. It was inspired by British prewar laws that aimed to keep guns away from colonists and was intended to ensure that citizens could protect themselves from government abuses.

Before the Revolutionary War, the British often required colonists to allow military personnel to live in their homes and eat their food. The **Third Amendment** prohibits this hated practice.

Amendments Four through Eight deal with the rights of people who are accused of committing crimes. The **Fourth Amendment*** requires a warrant (written permission from a judge) to search or confiscate (take) people's property.

The **Fifth Amendment** strengthens the Fourth Amendment, saying that no one can lose "life, liberty, or property" without a trial by jury. It prohibits "double jeopardy" (being tried twice for the same crime) and says that people cannot be compelled to testify if doing so might strengthen the case against them. This is known as "taking the Fifth." The Fifth Amendment also states that the government must compensate people fairly when it wants to use their land for a government or public purpose. This practice is often referred to as "eminent domain."

> * As stated above, the Townshend Act permitted British soldiers to search colonists' homes and businesses without a warrant. The American founders took this violation of privacy so seriously that they forbade it in the Fourth Amendment of the United States Constitution in 1789.

The **Sixth Amendment** guarantees an accused person's right to a speedy public trial with a judge and jury in the location where the crime occurred. Defendants must be allowed legal counsel (a lawyer), and they are allowed to call witnesses to testify on their behalf (in their favor). The **Seventh Amendment** says that civil lawsuits must be tried by a jury and that the judge cannot ignore what the jury says. The **Eighth Amendment** prohibits "cruel and unusual" punishment as well as excessive bail and fines.

The **Ninth** and **Tenth Amendments** say that states and individuals retain (keep) all rights that have not been specifically given to the federal government.

The Industrial Revolution (1760–1840)

The Industrial Revolution gets its name from the word **industry** (the process by which large machines turn raw materials like wood or cotton into completed furniture or clothing). Its advancements in technology created manufacturing jobs and enabled travel over greater distances, but they also made war more deadly and helped to prolong American slavery.

Inventions:

- **Textile Technology:** Two advances permitted people to weave cloth on an industrial scale for the first time in human history. The **flying shuttle** allowed a person to weave a wider piece of cloth, and the **spinning jenny** improved on old-fashioned spinning wheels by making it possible to spin more than one spindle (spool) of thread at a time. This made possible the weaving of cloth on an industrial scale.

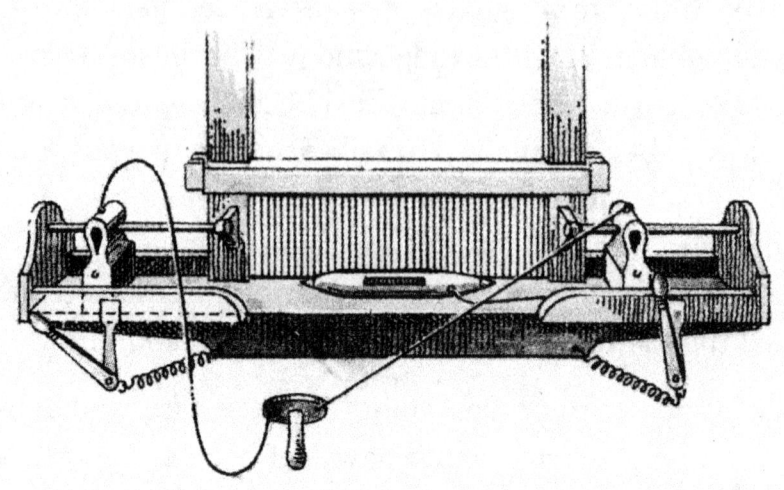

The flying shuttle allowed the creation of wider pieces of fabric. It produced cloth faster, especially once mechanized versions were built.

- **Power Loom:** Edmund Cartwright's 1784 invention revolutionized the British textile industry because it allowed each worker to produce cloth forty times faster than someone could by hand.

Spinning wheel.

Spinning jenny.

- **The Cotton Gin*** (1794): This machine quickly and easily separates cotton fibers from their seeds and was expected to reduce demand for enslaved workers because it increased the speed and efficiency of cleaning cotton. However, Northern factories' demand for cotton grew so quickly that more enslaved workers were forced to operate an ever-increasing number of cotton gins, cleaning ever larger quantities of cotton. Planters borrowed even more money to keep up with the demand. Over time, this meant that most slaveholding Southerners had little available cash, so they could not pay for necessities or pay the debts they already had.

* Although many people associate Eli Whitney's name with the cotton gin, there was an **SAT WRITING** passage about Catherine Green, who helped Whitney perfect the design and who was unfairly denied credit for her contribution.

Cotton Gin: Turning the crank turns wheels of comb-like spokes that clean seeds and debris from cotton fibers. Previously, seeds were combed out by hand, a slower and more labor-intensive process.

- **Trains:** The Newcomen steam engine, named for its creator, was invented in 1712. In 1769, James Watt patented the Watt steam engine, a faster, more efficient engine. Two of his steam engines began operating—one in England and one in Scotland—in 1776, the same year in which the Declaration of Independence was signed.

The first steam-powered train engine.

- **Telegraph:** American inventor **Samuel Morse** improved on the telegraph that had been invented in France. He constructed the first American telegraph line and invented **Morse code**, a system of short and long electric signals—dots and dashes—to send messages by telegraph. The United States Navy stopped using Morse code in the early 1970s, but some sailors still learn it.
- **Cement:** Although the ancient Romans invented concrete, the technology had been largely forgotten until an English bricklayer invented Portland cement, named for its resemblance to the limestone found on the British Isle of Portland. Others improved on his recipe, and cement is now one of the most important building materials worldwide.

- **Batteries:** Developed by Italian physicist **Alessandro Volta** (as in voltage), batteries were first mass-produced in 1802.
- **Dynamite:** Invented by **Alfred Nobel**, the Swiss chemist for whom the Nobel prizes are named, dynamite is better than gunpowder for exploding rock. Nobel believed his invention would only be used for peaceful projects like building roads and tunnels. He was wrong.
- **Photography:** The earliest surviving photograph was taken in 1826 by a French scientist, Joseph Nicéphore Niépce. Early photographs were also known as **daguerreotypes** after Louis Daguerre, who took the first photographs of people.

The oldest surviving photograph shows a view of the landscape surrounding Niépce's home.

- **Typewriter:** This American invention was at first called a typograph. A more efficient model was invented in 1867, and the QWERTY keyboard that we still use today was patented (registered with the government) in 1872.
- **Electric Generator:** The first electric generator was built in 1831. It was not very efficient, and better designs followed regularly.

- **Factory:** Factories replaced a "cottage industry" model in which textile workers worked at home and were paid on a per-piece basis. Now, people worked in a central location for wages, and this change led to radical social transformation.

  Factories provided jobs to people who had lost their land and could no longer farm for a living. People needed to live near the factories they worked in, so new urban areas were built to house them. However, the owners of these new factory towns were generally not interested in the welfare of their workers. Instead, they paid them as little as possible. Living conditions were overcrowded and dirty, work hours were long, and injuries were frequent. Workers were treated like disposable parts—if one was sick or injured, there was always another willing to take the job, sometimes even for lower pay. Women and children also worked. Women earned less than men, and children were paid least of all. Very young children were sometimes chained to machines to keep them from wandering. Kids who worked in the factories didn't get to go to school.

  Despite these drawbacks, cities continued to lure new workers. Changing economic and social conditions caused large numbers of people to move to the big cities and away from their small villages and families. Unsupervised and independent for the first time in their lives, they developed ideas and a sense of themselves as individuals. With money in their pockets, they participated in the life of the city and contributed to the rise of numerous occupations in the new manufacturing industries in textiles, pottery, paper, glass, and iron.

Adam Smith: Adam Smith was a Scottish philosopher and economist whose 1776 book, *An Inquiry into the Nature and Causes of* *the Wealth of Nations,* is regarded as a founding work of modern economic theory. Excerpts from it have appeared on SAT READING. Smith believed that reason leads people to act in their own self-interests, a tendency he called the "**invisible hand**." If the government allowed the "invisible hand" to guide economic activity instead of regulating it, the result would be national prosperity. The idea that governments should stay out of business is known as *laissez-faire* (**let it be**) **economics**, and it has remained an influential theory for over two hundred years.

The Wealth of Nations also explained Smith's idea that nations should calculate their wealth by using the **gross domestic product (GDP)** (the value of all goods and services produced in a year) instead of just looking at how much money they have in the bank or treasury. He also supported the **division of labor** because breaking a complex production process into individual steps that can be done by different people makes it faster and more efficient. This idea was particularly well-suited to the new factories of the Industrial Revolution.

The shift from an agricultural society to a manufacturing one did not please everyone, however. For example, SAT READING has used an essay by sociologist **John Ruskin** in which he argues that the division of labor dehumanizes workers by robbing them of creativity and the ability to take pride in their work. The **Luddites** were a group of independent weavers who tried to destroy the factory equipment that was threatening their livelihoods by producing cloth more quickly than they could by hand. Their attacks on factories sometimes led to violence. The movement dissolved after the British government passed a law proclaiming punishment by death for anyone damaging factory equipment. There have been SAT READING passages about clashes between the workers and owners of textile factories.

Transcendentalism: In the final decades of the eighteenth century, some Europeans and Americans rejected the Enlightenment's focus on reason and science. They worried that the Industrial Revolution was destroying the natural landscape and creating a way of life that replaced people with machines. In 1817, the British writer Mary Shelley* published *Frankenstein*, the first science fiction novel. In it, an overly ambitious scientist constructs a human-like creature from dead body parts and brings it to life with electricity. **SAT READING** has included selections of the first-person narrative of scientist Victor Frankenstein and that of his unnamed monster.

> *   Shelley's mother was British feminist** Mary Wollstonecraft, author of *A Vindication of the Rights of Woman*.

> **   Feminist: Someone who believes that men and women should have equal rights, privileges, and opportunities.

In the United States, the **Transcendentalist** movement believed in preserving nature and individual freedom. It opposed slavery and supported women's rights. **Ralph Waldo Emerson**, whose work often appears on **SAT READING**, believed that people should resist conformity (acting and thinking like everyone else) and trust their own perceptions instead. **Henry David Thoreau** criticized people for valuing possessions too much and advocated living simply, in harmony with nature. **Amos Bronson Alcott*** was an educator who opposed the harsh physical punishments that were common in schools at the time and advocated discussing material with students instead of simply requiring them to memorize facts. **Margaret Fuller** wrote *Woman in the Nineteenth Century*, in which she advocated for women's equality, and she became the first female overseas reporter for an American newspaper. Any of these writers could be used on SAT READING.

> * The father of Louisa May Alcott, an advocate of women's education who wrote *Little Women* and other popular nineteenth-century novels for young people.

The French Revolution (1789–1799)

Even more than the American Revolution, the French Revolution showed the power and promise of democratic government. It completely destroyed the social and political structures of the French *ancien régime* (old government) by abolishing the monarchy, outlawing feudalism, and rebuilding French society from the ground up. It also inspired the **Haitian Revolution**, a successful slave rebellion against French colonial rule that created the first black-led country in the Western Hemisphere. The French Revolution also led to the Reign of Terror and the Napoleonic Wars. All of this is discussed below.

A Brief History of France: France was first unified into one kingdom in the fifth century. It was governed by a monarch for about twelve hundred years, and it was a major world power from the sixteenth century until the end of World War II in 1945. In fact, France was so important that French was the *lingua franca* (dominant language) of business and politics just as English is today.

France and England were enemies for hundreds of years. The two countries fought twenty-eight separate wars between 1109 and the beginning of the **French Revolution** in 1789. Both the French and Indian War and French support of the American Revolutionary War were motivated by French hatred of the British.

The **Hundred Years, War** (1337–1453) resulted in three million (mostly French) deaths and a lot of destroyed French cities and towns. Ten years after the war started, the Bubonic plague (Black Death) arrived from Italy and killed about five million additional French people. In total, as much as half of France's population may have died from wars and plague.

In 1415, **King Henry V of England** defeated the French at the **Battle of Agincourt**, an event that William Shakespeare commemorated in his patriotic history play, *Henry V*. In 1428, French teenager **Joan of Arc** heard voices that she believed were from God. Guided by them, she dressed as a boy and traveled to see the French king, whom she convinced to allow her to lead French forces in combat. After several major victories, Joan was betrayed, captured, and burned alive at the stake by the English. She is considered a national hero in France and was canonized (made into a Catholic saint) in 1920.

France began building its empire in the sixteenth century, establishing colonies throughout the Americas. King Louis XIII legalized the sale of enslaved Africans domestically (at home in France) and abroad in France's colonies.

King Louis XIV won land and glory for France early in his reign (rule as king), earning the moniker (nickname), "the **Sun King**." A devout Catholic, he persecuted Huguenots (French Protestants), some of whom fled to colonies in North America. His near-constant warfare was expensive, he didn't invest in Industrial Revolution technology, and he left his country poorer and weaker than it had been at the outset of his reign.

Despite these problems, life in France improved throughout the eighteenth century. Medical advances and increasing prosperity allowed people to live longer. More babies survived as well, and the population nearly doubled. This strained the country's failure-prone agricultural system of small farms and increased hunger throughout France. At the same time, a new middle class of merchants and tradespeople—the *bourgeoisie*—wanted to have a say in government and for the nobility and clergy to pay their fair share of taxes. France's multiple European wars and its support of the American Revolutionary War were costly, and rising taxes fell disproportionately on the poor. Most of the nobility and clergy were exempt from paying any taxes at all.

It's important to remember that the Enlightenment was also taking place in the eighteenth century and that France was a hub of ideas and intellectual debate. The important Enlightenment philosophers **Jean Jacques Rousseau, Denis Diderot, Voltaire,** and the **Baron de Montesquieu** were all French, and their work (in translation) has been used for SAT READING history passages. Increasingly, people doubted the divine right of kings and believed that France needed a social contract that would create a more accountable, equitable (fair) form of government. When crop failures and high food prices in 1788 and 1789 created widespread hunger and discontent, conditions were ripe for revolution.

Louis XIV's grandson, **King Louis XVI** was a weak and unpopular monarch whose indecisiveness exacerbated (made worse) the political crisis caused by France's pecuniary (financial) problems. He married the Austrian princess **Marie Antoinette** to seal an alliance between Austria and France. Although the new French queen was beloved for her beauty and glamour at first, she was also distrusted because she was a foreigner. Her extravagant social life made her a symbol of the monarchy's wealth at a time when many ordinary French people were struggling to feed themselves and their families. As France's economic situation worsened, she became the symbol of everything that was wrong with the way French society was organized.

Forced to act by the food shortages and rising discontent, Louis XVI convened a meeting of the **Estates General**, a representative assembly of France's three "estates" (social classes). The First Estate represented the clergy, the Second Estate the nobility, and the Third Estate represented everyone else.

However, the Estates General had last met in 1614, and there were no rules for how the meetings should work or how disputes would be resolved. This led to chaos and controversy in 1789, when members of the Third Estate petitioned King Louis XVI to allow a one-man-one-vote policy that would prevent the more privileged First and Second Estates from outvoting the Third Estate two to one every time. Louis declined their request, so members of the Third Estate rebelled by founding the **National Assembly** to replace the Estates General.

At first, Louis appeared to accept that his power would now be limited by a new constitution. However, in June 1789, he ordered his officials to lock the National Assembly out of its meeting hall. Angry delegates then took possession of Louis's own indoor tennis court. In what is known as the "**Tennis Court Oath**," the delegates swore to remain until Louis agreed to let them write a new constitution. He did, but then, in a period known as the "**Great Fear**," he also began preparing troops to invade Paris, straining already stretched food supply chains with thousands of additional people to feed.

Storming of the Bastille (July 14, 1789): As prices and tensions rose in Paris, angry Parisians attacked a number of sites looking for food and weapons. One of these was the **Bastille**, a medieval fortress where arms and ammunition were stored and where a few political prisoners were kept. The storming (attacking) of the Bastille is generally seen as the start of the French Revolution. The prison governor was killed, and the mob celebrated by parading his head around on a spike. Bastille Day is a national holiday in France today.

Declaration of the Rights of Man: Just three weeks after the storming of the Bastille, the National Assembly adopted the **Declaration of the Rights of Man**, a document modeled on the American Declaration of Independence. It states that all people are born free and equal, with the rights to liberty and property ownership as well as the right to resist oppression and injustice. It guarantees freedom of speech, freedom of religion, and the right to bear arms and forbids arresting people without warrants. However, it did not emancipate (free) enslaved people or apply to women at all. This omission spurred responses from two prominent feminists: The French writer **Olympe de Gouges** published *The Declaration of the Rights of Woman and the Female Citizen* in 1791, and British feminist Mary Wollstonecraft published *A Vindication of the Rights of Woman* in 1792. Essays by De Gouges and Wollstonecraft have been used as history passages on SAT READING because their commitment to expanding women's rights is an important part of the story of democracy and human rights.

Women's March on Versailles: Just three months after the storming of the Bastille, angry women rioted because of food shortages and high prices. Joined by revolutionaries and others, the mob stormed the city armory and surrounded the palace at Versailles. The next day, they took the royal family into custody and forced them to return to Paris. After a failed escape attempt in 1791, the royal couple were tried by the revolutionary government and condemned to death by guillotine. Their sentences were carried out in 1793.

This drawing of two guillotines illustrates the efficiency with which this new device decapitated (cut the heads off) people.

Reign of Terror (1793–1794): By the fall of 1793, the French Revolution had stalled. Different revolutionary factions fought among themselves until a group led by **Maximilien de Robespierre** established a political dictatorship. It executed as many as seventeen thousand people, including aristocrats (members of the nobility) and anyone suspected of opposing the government. On some days, so many were executed that witnesses said "blood ran in the streets." In 1794, Robespierre and his allies were arrested by more moderate members of the revolutionary government and condemned to die by guillotine.

The French Revolution was greeted with excitement and alarm in England, where many feared a French invasion and a repeat of the Glorious Revolution (see above) that would overrule the English Bill of Rights to put a new absolute monarch on the throne. In 1790, the Irish politician **Edmund Burke** published "Reflections on the Revolution in France," in which he mourned the downfall of the French monarchy and worried about the Revolution's potential to become violent—which it did, during the **Reign of Terror.** Excerpts from Burke's "Reflections" in which he opposes the French Revolution have frequently appeared on SAT READING, often paired with more liberal writers such as Olympe de Gouges or Thomas Paine. Passages from novels set during the French Revolution, such as Charles Dickens's *A Tale of Two Cities* and Baroness Emmuska Orczy's play and novel, *The Scarlet Pimpernel*, have also been used as literature passages on SAT READING. If you get such a passage, your knowledge of the French Revolution will provide historical context that will help you identify main points, interpret context clues, and make correct inferences about tone and attitude.

Haitian Revolution (1791–1804): The French Revolution also inspired enslaved people in the French colonies. When Christopher Columbus claimed the Caribbean island of **Hispaniola** (the Spanish Isle) for Spain in 1492, its main inhabitants were the **Taíno,** who also populated many other Caribbean islands. Within twenty-five years, enslavement, disease, and murder reduced their population from over 500,000 to 32,000. Today, many Caribbean islanders carry Taíno DNA, and there has been increased historical interest in them and their culture. Passages about the **Taíno Genocide** (deliberate killing of most or all of a racial, ethnic, or religious group) have appeared on SAT WRITING.

In 1697, Spain gave the western third of Hispaniola to France, which named its new colony **Saint Domingo**. It soon became a flourishing plantation economy that enslaved about 500,000 Africans to raise sugar, cotton, coffee, and indigo (a plant that produces a valuable blue dye).

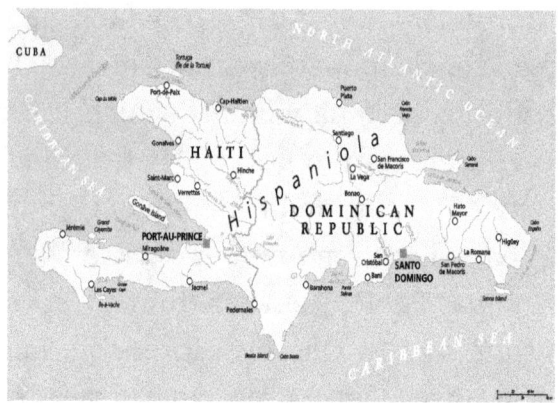

Slavery in Saint Domingo was a brutal affair. Africans arrived by the tens of thousands, but overwork, beatings, rapes, torture, disease, and murder meant that the enslaved population was always shrinking. Even so, new arrivals replaced those who died at such a rate that by 1789, the enslaved population was four times larger than the white one. Enslaved people responded to their poor treatment by running away in large numbers. Slave rebellions were frequent, and communities of former slaves, known as **maroons**, flourished in the island's jungles and fought their enslavers by attacking their homes and property, often by setting them on fire.

Toussaint L'Ouverture was born into slavery in Saint Domingo, but he was educated and spoke both French and Latin. He worked as an overseer of other enslaved people and was able to purchase his own freedom in 1776 or 1777. When a large slave rebellion began in 1791, he raised an army and became known for his ability to find openings* through enemy lines. He took over all of Hispaniola, ended slavery and ruled for two years before the French arrived, arrested him, and took him to France, where he died in prison. His revolution survived, however, because another leader, **Jean-Jacques Dessalines**, pushed the French out and established the first black republic, Haiti. L'Ouverture's successful rebellion terrified slave holders in the United States and caused them to respond to the smallest act of slave defiance with extreme violence.

> * Toussaint adopted L'Ouverture as his last name because it means "the opening" in French.

Nineteenth-Century Europe (1800–1914)

Napoleonic Wars: For five years after Robespierre's downfall, France struggled economically while also attempting to conduct several wars, including against the British. During this time, France was ruled by a group of committees. In 1798, French General **Napoléon Bonaparte** led a *coup d'état* (a takeover of government by force), became the new leader of the French government, and began conquering large portions of Europe. In between military victories, he rewrote France's legal code so that the laws applied to everyone, centralized the French government, and built many *lycées* (secondary schools) for boys.

The Napoleonic Wars immersed Europe in ten devastating years of total war* that ended in 1815. These wars had long-term consequences for the United States as well because Napoléon financed his wars by selling the **Louisiana Territory** to the United States in 1803. The land that the United States acquired by this purchase opened the door to westward expansion in the nineteenth century, and his war with Britain distracted its attention from the War of 1812.

> ✳ Total War: When a society uses its entire military and all civilian resources to wage war and prioritizes (chooses) the war effort over the welfare of civilians.

In 1812, Napoléon was defeated by the British, who exiled him to a small Mediterranean island. He escaped, returned to power, resumed waging war, and was finally defeated by the British in the **Battle of Waterloo in 1815**. The phrase "to meet one's Waterloo" has come to mean that someone suffered a final defeat.

European Peace: After Napoléon's defeat in the Battle of Waterloo, representatives from the victorious countries (England, Russia, Prussia*, and Austria) gathered at the **Congress of Vienna** to redraw the map of Europe to suit themselves. Small, weak countries and disputed territories were bargained over. It was all very complicated, but the result was a well-balanced Europe in which all the major powers were roughly equal. The result was a forty-year peace that made it possible for England to expand its empire and become a major world power.

> ✳ Prussia was the strongest Germanic kingdom until the end of World War I, when it became a state in the Weimar Republic of Germany.

However, European peace did not mean that European leaders trusted one another. Many nations made treaties in which they promised to come to the other's aid if attacked. A century later, these mutual aid agreements pulled many countries into a regional conflict in the Austrian Empire and ignited World War I.

The Congress of Vienna changed the lives of many Europeans in unintended ways. For example, Russia gave Poland to Austria in exchange for Galicia (which no longer exists) without consulting the people of either place, and this set the stage for revolutions, migration to the United States, and eventually to World War I.

Economic Disruption: At the same time, the Industrial Revolution was changing how people lived and worked. Europe and the United States suffered from increasing income inequality as the Industrial Revolution pulled people from farms to work in factories for low wages.

Laborers experienced ongoing hardships from long hours, poor conditions, and low pay. Factory owners and overseers were not obligated (required) to make their factories safe or pleasant to work in, and there were no laws restricting how many hours people could be required to work. There was no minimum wage, and employers could reduce wages with impunity (without consequence). There was no health insurance or sick leave, and employers did not have to care if people were injured on the job because there were always new workers available. For millions, life was an endless cycle of work and sleep.

Child labor was prevalent (common) in Europe and the United States in the nineteenth century, and many children never learned to read or write. Poor people could not support children who did not contribute to the family income, so children worked on farms, in factories, and even in mines. In cities, boys sold newspapers, delivered messages, and shined shoes. Girls worked as shop assistants, domestic laborers, and prostitutes. Many children had only one or two years of schooling before poverty forced them into low-paying jobs.

Educators responded to the new lifestyles and livelihoods of the Industrial Revolution in both the United States and Europe by calling for all children to attend school. There, they would learn how to be good workers and good citizens. ON SAT READING, you may encounter a passage or set of paired passages by nineteenth century writers who see children as human "resources" or "materials." These writers saw children as future workers who needed to learn to do as they were told, whereas others wanted education to be more focused on developing the potential of each student. The British novelist Charles Dickens is known for his sympathetic portrayals of poor children, and his novel *Hard Times* contains a school superintendent whose pedagogy (educational approach) focuses on memorizing useless facts. Passages from many of Dickens's novels have appeared on SAT READING.

Russia: Russia did not industrialize as fast as the rest of Europe. The country's vast size made it difficult to travel, communicate, or develop urban centers for industry and manufacturing. If you couldn't sail there on a river, you had to either walk or ride a horse or donkey. There were enormous forests filled with bears and wolves, and the winters were long, hard, and cold. Also, much of the country's agricultural produce came from large estates that were owned by members of the Russian nobility and farmed by serfs. Interestingly, Russian serfs were finally freed in 1861. American slaves were freed in 1865.

Freeing the serfs created new problems in Russia because suddenly freeing over twenty million people meant that they needed a way to earn a living. Those who remained farmers were now required to pay extremely high taxes. People who migrated to cities for factory work often found that their working conditions were terrible and that their pay was too low to live on. Inequality persisted and the poor suffered, leading to a failed revolution in 1905 and a successful one in 1917 (more on that later).

Marxism: The 1840s were a time of widespread hunger and poverty throughout Europe. German philosopher, economist, and journalist **Karl Marx** became motivated to search for the root causes of these social ills. He concluded that they stemmed from class inequality that resulted from the division of society into capital (owners) and labor (workers).

The German authorities understood Marx's ideas as a direct threat to their wealth and power. They did not want a radical writer to get people stirred up with ideas about equality and democracy. To avoid trouble and possible arrest, Marx fled to England. In February 1848, he and his philosopher friend **Friedrich Engels** published *The Communist Manifesto*. This important book inspired the communist revolutions of the nineteenth and twentieth centuries in Europe, Asia, and the Americas. Its influence continues to shape geopolitics (world politics) and economic theory today. As with the French Revolution, you should know the basics so that you understand how later writers used communist theories in their own work.

The Communist Manifesto argues that the struggle among the social classes (aristocracy, church, peasants, and serfs) is the supreme struggle that defines human history. It says that income inequality exists because the rich own "the means of production," meaning the factories, farms, railroads and other infrastructure, and they will do anything to hold onto their property and power. Marx and Engels also argue that workers will always be poor because owners will always pay them as little as they can get away with. They predict that income inequality will eventually get so bad that the "workers of the world" will unite in a violent revolution to overthrow their harsh overlords (kings, czars, and other enemies of "the people").

After studying the urban working poor in England, Marx concluded that the workers' revolution would take place first in the industrialized nations: France, Germany, England, and the United States. He believed that after a short period of authoritarian rule that he called the "dictatorship of the **proletariat**" (rule by working class people), an elected government would take over and manage the economy. All banks, factories, farms, and transportation networks would be publicly owned. The government's job would be to divide it all fairly so that everyone got what they needed to live a reasonably decent life (no starvation or homelessness).

However, the revolution Marx predicted did not take place in the industrialized countries of western Europe or the United States. Instead, it occurred in underdeveloped Russia. Some historians argue that the democratic systems of western Europe simply absorbed potential revolutionaries by letting them run for political office and express their opinions in the free press. Russia was ruled by an autocratic leader called the **czar**. He had complete control over the economy, the military and the church. As in pre-revolutionary France, extreme income inequality and the lavish lifestyles of the aristocracy and clergy created the conditions for widespread social unrest.

Irish Potato Famine (1845–1852): The deadliest famine in nineteenth-century Europe was caused by *Phytophthora infestans* (or *P. infestans*), a mold that grows on wet leaves. When it infects potato plants, it kills them.

The British began colonizing Ireland in the twelfth century, and Irish resistance to British rule began at the same time. England treated Ireland like a colony and exploited its resources by requiring much of the food it produced to be exported to England for consumption. The Protestant British looked down on the Catholic Irish and sought to treat them as second-class workers whose role was to enrich England. Most of the Irish landowning aristocracy was either English or Anglo-Irish (English-Irish), and most Irish Catholics remained landless tenant farmers.

When the famine began in Ireland, the British response was ineffective at best, but many Irish saw it as a deliberate attempt at genocide. Over a seven-year period during which Irish food exports to England increased, over one million Irish people died of starvation, malnutrition and disease. At the same time, eyewitnesses reported seeing bodies lying along the road with mouths stained green from eating grass.

The combined impact of forced food exports and the deaths of more than one-tenth of Ireland's population energized the Irish nationalist* movement and began over one hundred years of organized Irish resistance to British rule. It also started a flood of emigration (leaving one's home country) that reduced Ireland's population by about 50 percent by 1921. Most of those who left emigrated to the United States.

> * Nationalism is the belief that one's nation is superior to all others. Nationalists often view other nations as rivals and inferiors. They may also believe that their country has the right to rule others.

Revolutions of 1848: An economic depression left many Europeans feeling disenchanted (unhappy) with their lives. People wanted a more democratic government and more guarantees of human rights. Ethnic minorities who had lost their homelands as a result of the Congress of Vienna wanted independence and self-determination (the right to choose their own government). The first revolution took place in Sicily, and others followed in Italy, Germany, France, and the Austrian Empire. The revolutions did not achieve their goals, and many people felt that their future was bleak. Others also feared being targeted by their governments for taking part in the unrest or for belonging to minority groups. Taken together, these events contributed to a steady flow of immigrants to the United States.

Crimean War (1853–1856): The Crimean War was sparked by religious tensions between Catholics and the Orthodox believers, including Russians, over access to Jerusalem and other places considered sacred by Christians under Turkish rule.

The **Russian Empire** lost to a coalition of the Ottoman Empire, Britain, France, and Sardinia (which became part of Italy in 1861), undermining Russian influence in Europe. The Crimean War was the first war in which telegraphs, an Industrial Revolution invention, were used to report news straight from the battlefront. For the first time, readers could read about battles that took place only hours earlier. A British nurse, **Florence Nightingale**, invented modern nursing (including the idea that nursing was an acceptable occupation for women) during this war, and passages about the development of nursing have appeared as SAT READING passages.

Boer* Wars: The Boer Wars were two conflicts in South Africa that took place between 1899 and 1902 between the British and the Dutch over land that was inhabited by black Africans because rich deposits of diamonds and other minerals had been found on it. Neither colonizer took the presence of those Africans very seriously because they saw them as uncivilized primitives who would be easy to control and profit from. The British won and agreed that the defeated Boers could form a new nation, the Republic of South Africa. In 1910, South Africa became a part of the British Empire.

> * The Boers are descended from seventeenth-century Dutch** colonizers of South Africa.

> ** The Dutch are residents of the **Netherlands**, which is sometimes incorrectly called Holland. Holland is actually only one of the Netherlands' twelve provinces.

In England, an entire generation of young men was inspired by the stories about the glory and honor that had been won in South Africa, and many volunteered enthusiastically to fight in World War I when it began in 1914. However, it is important to know that during the Boer Wars the British army under **Lord Kitchener** conducted a brutal scorched earth campaign against its opponents, complete with segregated concentration camps to separate white Boer refugees from their darker-skinned allies of African descent.

Nineteenth-Century United States (1800–1860)

President Thomas Jefferson's 1803 **Louisiana Purchase** doubled the size of the United States and added invaluable (extremely useful) natural resources and people to the United States, including Native American tribes and French settlers who lived in and around New Orleans.

The Louisiana Purchase doubled the size of the United States.

War of 1812: After the American Revolution, the United States was drawn into a second war with England for reasons that were directly related to the ongoing hostilities between France and England. It was also complicated by the United States' expansion into the land acquired after the Louisiana Purchase because the Native Americans they were displacing fought on the side of the British.

The British and the French wanted to prevent each other from trading with the United States. Privateers (private ships working for the government) from both sides stopped American ships, searched them and sometimes confiscated (took) their cargo. In addition, British Navy ships sometimes "impressed" (forced)

American sailors and passengers into working for them on their ships. A "press gang" is a group of impressed sailors.

The United States responded by declaring war on Great Britain in June 1812, and the city of Detroit surrendered to the British two months later. Numerous battles were fought on land and at sea. In 1814, British troops entered Washington, DC, and burned down the White House.

The War of 1812 ended in 1814 when the **Treaty of Ghent** was signed in Belgium, and it began a period of peace and mutual prosperity for the United States, England, and Canada. However, news that the war was over did not reach New Orleans in time to prevent the **Battle of New Orleans** in January 1815, in which a small American force defeated a much larger British one.

Monroe Doctrine (1823): Named for **President James Monroe**, this doctrine says that the United States opposes European attempts to colonize or control any independent countries in the western hemisphere (North America, Central America, and South America). It also says that the United States will not become involved in the affairs of the eastern hemisphere (Africa, Asia, Australia, and Europe). The **Monroe Doctrine** expresses the United States' declaration of support for the new republics of Mexico, Argentina, Colombia, Chile, and Peru, all former Spanish colonies, and it continues to play a role in United States' foreign policy today. President Monroe announced the doctrine during his 1823 State of the Union speech, which could be used as an SAT READING passage.

EXPANSION!
The western patrol's long stretch.

Uncle Sam* stands with one foot on each continent, armed with a club ready to repel European attackers.

> * The image of Uncle Sam has represented the United States since 1813 and could easily be a passage topic for SAT WRITING.

Alexis de Tocqueville: A French political scientist and sociologist, Tocqueville published *Democracy in America* after traveling the United States in the early 1830s. He believed that democracy was an "unstoppable force" because it treated all people as equal before the law. He noted the irony of slavery in a democracy based on equality and predicted that rights would gradually be extended to minority groups. He also worried that a government based on the majority rule was in danger of persecuting minority groups and that too strong a belief in individual liberty could prove detrimental (harmful) to the good of the community. His book is still regarded as one of the best analyses of nineteenth-century American society, and multiple excerpts from it have appeared on SAT READING.

Indian Removal Act: Since the end of the American Revolutionary War, the United States had treated the **Indian Nations** as sovereign states with which it could negotiate, trade, and cooperate. However, conflict between individual settlements and tribes continued throughout the nineteenth century as white Americans ventured farther south and west.

In 1830, President Andrew Jackson broke with established United States policy and signed the **Indian Removal Act**, which authorized the government to trade land west of the Mississippi River for land in the southeastern states that could be devoted to cotton plantations. He and his successor, **President Martin van Buren**, used military force to remove southeastern Native American tribes from their land if they did not leave voluntarily.

In 1836, 15,000 Creek Indians were relocated from Alabama to Oklahoma; only about 12,000 survived the trip. Two years later, in a forced march known as the **Trail of Tears**, over 100,000 men, women and children were forced to march 5,000 miles from the southeast to newly allocated (set aside) "Indian Territory" west of the Mississippi River. At least 15,000 thousand people died of starvation and sickness. In general, throughout the eighteenth and nineteenth centuries, the land that the Indian Nations were given was smaller and less hospitable than the land they had been forced to leave.

Texan Independence (1836–1846): When Mexico gained its independence from Spain in 1821, it encouraged white Americans to settle on its large areas of unclaimed land in the northern state of **Coahuila-Tejas** (one of the states of the newly established United Mexican States). It also outlawed slavery. Within a few years, white Americans outnumbered Mexicans, whom they saw as racially inferior to whites. In 1830, Mexico ended immigration from the United States. An independence movement developed among white settlers and gained the support of pro-slavery Americans in Texas.

The new Mexican government was modeled on that of the United States. However, **General Antonio López de Santa Anna** overthrew the new government and became Mexico's dictator. When Texas, which was part of Mexico, opposed his rule, he led an invasion force of six thousand soldiers into Texas.

The most famous battle in the War of Texas Independence was the 1836 **Battle of the Alamo** in which two hundred Texans died defending the Alamo, a Spanish fort in San Antonio, Texas, against almost two thousand Mexican troops. The Texans were led by **James Bowie*** and **Davy Crockett.**

> * Bowie's brother Rezin designed the Bowie knife, which James made famous when he killed an opponent with one in a fight.

For most of the twentieth century, American students were taught that the Americans' willingness to die defending Texas against a Mexican dictator was proof of the United States' commitment to freedom and democracy*. In the last few decades, however, that interpretation has been challenged by evidence that shows that the white heroes of the Alamo were slaveholders opposed to Mexico's anti-slavery laws. They also didn't fight alone. Mexican *Tejanos* (Texans) were among the defenders at the Alamo, often with their families, but their presence is often omitted from American history textbooks.

> * This incomplete version of the story was in my fifth-grade social studies textbook in the mid-1970s.

Historians have also learned that not all the defenders of the Alamo died. Women and children at the fort surrendered, and there is even evidence that Davy Crockett did not die in battle, but instead was captured and executed as a prisoner of war. Finally, Native Americans want acknowledgement that the Spanish built the Alamo on a sacred burial ground. Native Americans and Mexican Americans have long viewed the Alamo as a symbol of Spanish oppression and American aggression.

Mexican-American War (1846–1848): The United States captured the Mexican state of Texas and designated it a slave state in 1845. However, Mexico and the United States did not agree on Texas's actual borders, and war broke out. The United States won the war and kept Texas as well as all or parts of Arizona, California, Colorado, Nevada, New Mexico, Utah, and Wyoming. At the same time, many newly arrived European immigrants took advantage of the federal government's offer of free land in its newly acquired western territories. The 1862 **Homestead Act** granted 160 acres of public land to anyone who could live on and farm it for five years.

The United States government wanted to ensure that its new lands would be populated primarily by white people of European descent. In 1845, the term **Manifest* Destiny** became a convenient way of expressing the idea that God wanted white people to displace non-white indigenous (native) people as well as people of mixed Spanish-native ancestry.

* Manifest means "obvious" or "clear." The term implies that coast-to-coast expansion is obviously God's plan for the United States.

Manifest Destiny personified as a white woman.

When gold was discovered in California in 1848, the white population in the state increased from about 20,000 to about 100,000 by the end of 1849. This influx intensified the United States' effort to eradicate Native Americans. Both national and state authorities encouraged and financed the murder, rape, and enslavement of California's Native American population in what's known as the **California Genocide**. Mexicans who lived in territory that the United States won in the Mexican-American War were also targeted for violence and driven from their land.

Prelude to Civil War: The northern United States remained largely white after the end of the American Revolution. In about 1830, immigration increased as many Europeans fled poverty or persecution in their home countries. Most of these immigrants either remained in the North to work in manufacturing or headed west to claim land for farming. Only a few traveled south since there were fewer economic opportunities there and because most jobs were already performed by enslaved people.

In contrast, the South had a white population committed to enslaving a larger population of Africans and African Americans. White Southerners feared the anger of the people they treated harshly, so they did not hesitate to respond violently whenever they felt threatened. Every failed slave rebellion—and they all failed—in the United States ended in an excessive bout (outbreak) of white violence against the rebels and suspected sympathizers. Also, since the South's energy and money was tied up in perpetuating (continuing) slavery, it didn't develop a significant manufacturing base or even build an extensive system of railroad tracks for the new trains that were beginning to crisscross the countryside. As a result, it was less prepared to go to war than the North was when the Civil War began.

The successful 1791 Haitian slave uprising (above) terrified slave-holding Americans, as did Nat Turner's 1831 rebellion, in which 51 white people were murdered. The white community retaliated (responded) with even more violence—56 enslaved people, not all of whom took part in the rebellion, were executed, and about another 120 uninvolved black people were murdered in the surrounding area by local militias (armed groups of civilians) or mobs.

Mason-Dixon Line: In 1763, Charles Mason and Jeremiah Dixon surveyed the boundary between the then-British colonies, Pennsylvania and Maryland. Decades later, the **Mason-Dixon Line** became known as the border between Southern "slave states" and their Northern "free state" neighbors who opposed slavery. If an SAT READING passage refers to the Mason-Dixon Line, you only need to remember that north of the line was free territory, and that south was territory where slavery was legal and encouraged.

Fugitive Slave Acts: The **First Fugitive Slave Act** was passed in 1793. It said that local governments were empowered to catch and return runaway slaves to their owners. The **Second Fugitive Slave Act** was passed in 1850, and it stipulated (said) that African Americans who escaped slavery were still slaves, even if they were free in the state they escaped to. In practice, this meant that any black person could be called an escaped slave. In 1853, **Solomon Northup**, who was born free, was kidnapped and sold into twelve years of brutal slavery. Northup's memoir, *Twelve Years a Slave*, was made into a movie in 2013.

Many of the American founders thought that slavery could be allowed to die out naturally, although how this would happen was never fully explained. The Northern states all outlawed it by 1804, and Congress outlawed importing newly-enslaved Africans in 1807. However, this law was ineffective at reducing slavery because there were already enough slaves in the United States to be a self-sustaining population. It also did not impact the state-to-state slave trade. Finally, since there was still a demand for newly enslaved Africans, a pirate trade sprang up to fill it. As more states were admitted to the United States, the status of each state as a "slave state" or a "free state" became political as the defenders and opponents of slavery each sought to gain an advantage.

Missouri Compromise: In 1820, the United States Congress passed a law that admitted Missouri to the "union" of the United States as a slave state and Maine as a free state. It also said that all new lands north of the green line on the map below would outlaw slavery while those below the green line permitted slavery. Oklahoma, which was still just a territory, began permitting slavery in the 1830s. Keep in mind, however, that the Missouri Compromise line and the Mason-Dixon Line (above) are not the same even though they were both used to divide states by whether or not they permitted slavery.

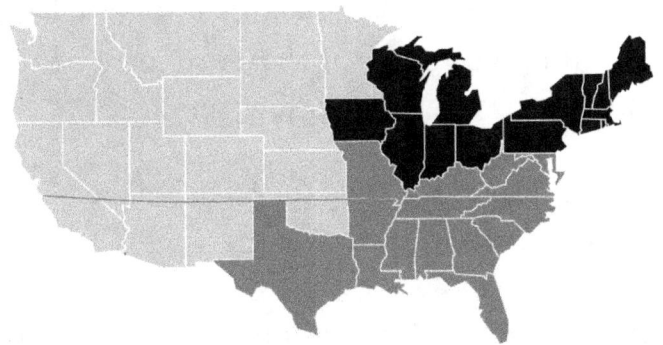

Under the Missouri Compromise, every place north of the green line would become a free state, and everywhere south of the line would become a slave state.

Underground Railroad: Neither an actual train nor underground, the Underground Railroad was a loosely organized network of abolitionists who helped runaways escape from slavery to freedom in the Northern United States. Once the 1850 Fugitive Slave Act allowed escaped slaves to be captured in the free Northern states and returned to their owners, the volunteer "conductors" on the Underground Railroad helped over thirty thousand runaways cross the border to Canada, where slavery was illegal. Homemade quilts stitched with secret, coded messages for runaways played an important role in the history and folklore of the Underground Railroad, and historical articles about these quilts and the women who stitched them could be selected for SAT WRITING.

Harriet Tubman: Born enslaved in Maryland in 1822, **Harriet Tubman** endured a brutal childhood before escaping in 1849. Tubman is famous for escaping slavery and returning south multiple times to lead enslaved people to freedom on the Underground Railroad, a feat for which she became known as "Moses"*. During the Civil War, she served the Union as a nurse, soldier and spy and became the first woman to lead a combat mission. However, since women were prohibited from joining the armed forces, she was denied payment and veteran's benefits. Her claims went unrecognized for thirty-four years before she was finally granted a small pension for her services.

> *   In the Bible, Moses leads the Jewish people out of slavery in Egypt.

Missouri Compromise of 1850: Congress passed this series of five bills to resolve fierce debate about whether the territories that the United States had won in the Mexican-American war should become slave states when they gained statehood. The bills strengthened fugitive slave laws, kept slavery legal in Washington, DC, and admitted California as a free state. However, the Compromise did not resolve debates about slavery in United States territories that wanted to become states.

Bleeding Kansas (1854–1861): Many historians see the violence over slavery that occurred in Kansas as a localized civil war that presaged (foreshadowed) the national civil war. Under the Missouri Compromise, both Nebraska and Kansas would have become free states. Most Nebraskans were against slavery, as were most Kansans, but many Southerners were eager to claim Kansas, bordered by the slave states of Missouri and Oklahoma, for slavery.

Pro-slavery **Senator Stephen Douglas** of Illinois introduced the **Kansas-Nebraska Act** in Congress to support such efforts at the national level. When the Act became law, it repealed (overturned) the Missouri Compromise and said the voters would decide the slave or free status of their new state. Another slavery supporter, **Senator David Atchison** of Missouri, led thousands of Missourians over the Kansas border, where their illegal votes helped to make Kansas a slave state in 1854.

In response, abolitionists founded the town of Lawrence, Kansas, and used it as a base for their anti-slavery efforts. Violence between residents and members of a pro-slavery encampment led to an armed standoff and two deaths in November, 1855.

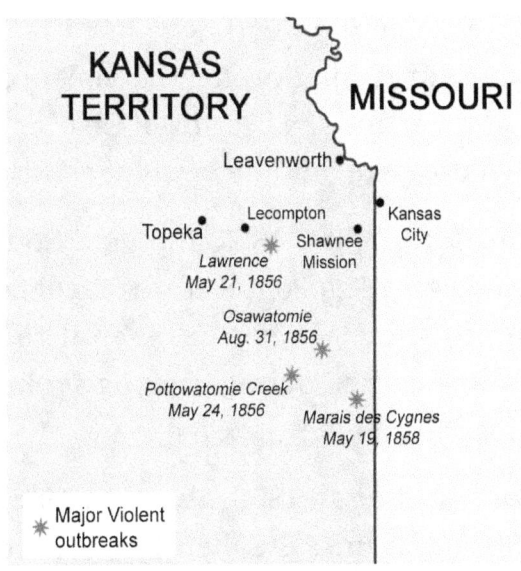

The 1854 border between Missouri and the Kansas Territory.

The month of May, 1856, stands out for a series of events that moved the United States closer to civil war. On May 19 and 20, **Senator Charles Sumner** delivered a five-hour speech that denounced the Kansas-Nebraska Act and targeted both its originator Senator Douglas and South Carolina **Senator Andrew Butler** for insults and attacks on their personal morals. In a passage that has been used on SAT READING, he calls the Kansas-Nebraska act a "swindle" (cheat) and calls slavery "an arrogant denial of human rights" far greater than anything suffered by slaveholders who lose their right to enslave others.

On May 22, Senator Butler's nephew, **Congressman Preston Brooks**, attacked Senator Sumner with a walking cane and beat him nearly to death in front of a number of other politicians.

Brooks planned the attack as retaliation for the insults Sumner had leveled at Butler.

Pottawatomie Massacre: On May 24, the militant white abolitionist **John Brown** led a small group, including his five sons, to a pro-slavery settlement on Pottawatomie Creek, where they murdered five men in retaliation for the violence in Lawrence the previous November and the beating of Charles Sumner. After the attack, Brown escaped, but one of his sons was killed.

Dred Scott v. Sandford: The 1857 Supreme Court decision in the case of *Dred Scott v. Sandford* said that federal law did not grant citizenship to any black person, even if that person was born free. The ruling caused outrage among abolitionists, but it was not overturned until after the Civil War.

Lincoln-Douglas Debates: In 1858, **Abraham Lincoln** ran for the United States Senate against Stephen Douglas, the sponsor of the Kansas-Nebraska Act. The two candidates participated in a series of seven debates about the morality of slavery and states' rights to decide for themselves if they wanted to permit it within their borders. These debates are frequently excerpted as paired passages on SAT READING. Lincoln opposed slavery and said the country could not survive "half-slave and half-free" and that a "house divided against itself cannot stand." Douglas, in contrast, argued that the country had done perfectly well divided and that there was no good reason not to continue slavery in those states that wanted it. Although Lincoln lost the Senate race, he won the presidency two years later.

Raid on Harpers Ferry (1859): John Brown led an attack on the United States armory, arsenal and rifle facility in Harpers Ferry, Virginia*. He and his followers, both black and white, held the armory for about thirty-six hours before being forced to flee. In the end, Brown and six of his surviving men were executed on charges of treason (betrayal of their country), murder, and insurrection (rebellion).

> * Today, Harpers Ferry is in West Virginia. The state was created in 1863, when the western part of Virginia rejected secession and chose to ally itself with the Union.

The Raid on Harpers Ferry and John Brown's death were among the most hotly debated issues of the 1860 presidential election. Abolitionists hailed Brown as a martyr (hero who dies for a cause), but many white Southerners became convinced that all abolitionists were violent religious fanatics.

Abolitionist Literature: In 1789, **Olaudah Equiano** published the first slave narrative, *Interesting Narrative of the Life of Olaudah Equiano, or Gustavus Vassa, the African.* Published in England, Equiano's autobiography describes his West African boyhood, abduction, enslavement in England and eventual freedom. The book influenced the 1833 abolition of slavery in England.

A number of formerly enslaved African Americans, including **Frederick Douglass, Sojourner Truth, Harriet Jacobs,** and Solomon Northup, also published accounts of their lives in slavery. These slave narratives spoke bluntly about the brutality and horror of slavery, and they became powerful tools for the abolitionist cause. Multiple passages from their writing have appeared on SAT READING.

African American Newspapers: In 1827, *Freedom's Journal,* the first newspaper that was owned and operated by African Americans, began publishing a weekly newsletter that covered current events and politics and openly opposed slavery. Other black-owned newspapers sprang up over the next several decades. An article or editorial by a prominent black abolitionist could be used on SAT READING.

White Abolitionists' Writings: Abolitionist feelings also grew steadily among white people, especially in the North. In 1831, **William Lloyd Garrison** founded *The Liberator*, an abolitionist magazine, and an SAT READING passage could be taken from an article his magazine published. A white writer, **Harriet Beecher Stowe**, published *Uncle Tom's Cabin; or, Life among the Lowly* as a series of magazine installments in 1851–1852, and it did more to advance the cause of abolition than any other individual text. When the completed book was finally published, the first 300,000 copies sold out in less than three months, and it's often referred to by other nineteenth-century writers.

Two other prominent white abolitionists whose writing has been used for SAT READING passages were **Sarah and Angelina Grimke.** Born to a slaveholding family in South Carolina, they rebelled against their family's exploitation of enslaved people as well as against the limitations that were placed on women's behavior in the nineteenth century. They moved to Philadelphia, where they spoke and wrote for the abolitionist cause. They also wrote about their defiance of the social convention (custom) that said women should not speak in public and argued that it was more important to do the right thing than it was to be ladylike.

Although many black and white abolitionists were religious Christians who saw slavery as antithetical (opposed) to God's will as it is expressed in the Bible, many **pro-slavery writers** also based their arguments on sections of the Bible that describe the treatment of slaves in ancient Israel. These pro-slavery texts portray slavery as a family-like arrangement in which happy slaves love their owners, who always have their slaves' best interests at heart. Pro-slavery writers used euphemisms (nicer ways of saying blunt truths) to describe slavery, calling it the "peculiar institution," and calling slaves "servants."

The American Civil War (1860–1865)

The American Civil War included over ten thousand military encounters and about 150 significant battles, but don't panic. You only need to know a few of the most significant. Many Civil War battles have two names—a Southern one and a Northern one. In general, the Union army named battles after nearby rivers and streams, while the Confederate army used the names of nearby towns.

President Lincoln took office in March 1861. His first inaugural address* was a plea to maintain the Union. He said that the Fugitive Slave Acts were still in full force and that no one wanted to strip white Southerners of their right to enslave black people.

> * An inauguration is the swearing-in ceremony for a new president. It includes an inaugural address (speech) by the new president. Lincoln was elected twice, so he had two inaugural addresses.

Southern Secession: Almost immediately, South Carolina seceded (separated) from the rest of the United States. Six other slaveholding states joined it to the form the Confederate States of America, a new country that permitted slavery. Ultimately, eleven states made up the Confederacy, and twenty-five states remained in the "Union," a term that Northerners preferred because it emphasized the idea that the states united to form one country. **Jefferson Davis**, who represented Mississippi in the United States Senate and House of Representatives before the American Civil War, was elected president of the Confederate States in 1861, and he held that position until the South's surrender in 1865.

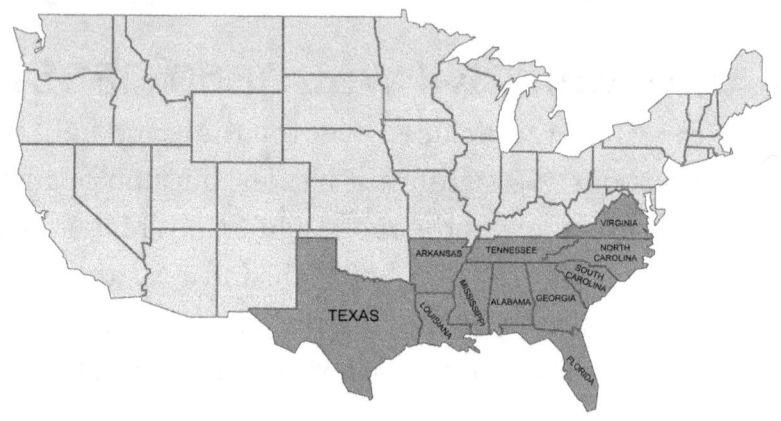

The Confederate States of America.

The **American Civil War** remains the deadliest conflict in American history, with over six hundred thousand deaths. Historians often call it the first modern war because it was the first armed conflict in which the new technologies of the Industrial Revolution played a major role. Nineteenth-century rifles shot farther and more accurately than the muskets of the Revolutionary War. The invention of the telegraph meant that commanders could communicate over great distances to coordinate their strategy. Trains hauled men, munitions and supplies faster and with greater ease than had ever been possible before. Steam-propelled ships sported new iron hulls (main body of a ship) that were more resistant to torpedoes and fire than wooden hulls; torpedoes that could pierce them were also invented. Land mines, hand grenades and submarines provided new opportunities to

inflict mass damage, and hot air balloons made airborne recon-
naissance a vital new intelligence tool.

All this new technology affected not only how the Civil War was
fought, but also how it was recorded and written about. Photography could show people what war really looked like, and reporters could telegraph their stories from the front line in time for
the next day's newspaper.

At the start of the Civil War, the Union produced more than the
Confederacy in virtually every area of the economy. Northern
states had more railroads and manufacturing, and they could
easily mass-produce standardized weapons with interchange-
able parts and ship them to Union troops throughout the country. Furthermore, all men who were eligible to be soldiers were
free in the North, whereas large numbers of Southern men were
en- slaved and could not be expected to fight against their own
lib- eration. Also, some white men needed to stay home to prevent slave rebellions.

The North's clear technological and numerical advantages made
it overconfident of victory, and this attitude, combined with
poor military leadership, caused the North to lose every Civil
War battle in the early days of the war.

The Civil War began about six weeks after the Southern states
seceded. South Carolina militia fired on federal troops stationed
at **Fort Sumter** and forced their surrender. President Lincoln issued a call for 75,000 volunteers to fight. He mistakenly thought
it would only take about three months to defeat the Confederacy and return the seceding states to the Union. He also initi-
ated the **Union Blockade**, in which Union ships patrolled more
than 3,500 miles of the Atlantic and Gulf coasts to prevent the
Confederacy from engaging in overseas trade with England and

other countries. The Union Blockade continued until the end of the war four years later.

The Battles of Bull Run* (1861): The **First Battle of Bull Run** was a major victory for the South. Bull Run is in Virginia, and Union troops beat a hasty retreat back to Washington, DC. The Union suffered a similarly embarrassing defeat at the **Second Battle of Bull Run.**

> * The Confederate names for the two battles are the First and Second Battles of Manassas.

Battle of Antietam* (1862): The Battle of Antietam was the single deadliest day of the war: about 25,000 casualties (wounded) and 3,600 deaths. Although it was militarily inconclusive (no clear winner), it caused England and France to rescind (take back) their offers to recognize the Confederate States of America as a legitimate country.

> * The Confederate name is the Battle of Sharpsburg.

Emancipation Proclamation (January 1, 1863): The diplomatic victory that followed the Battle of Antietam led Lincoln to issue the **Emancipation Proclamation,** which said that all enslaved people in the South were now free. However, slavery did not end in the South until June 19, 1865, when a United States Army officer read "General Order No. 3" aloud in Galveston, Texas, to the last group of enslaved people. June 19 later became known as **"Juneteenth"** and was celebrated by African Americans as a holiday to commemorate the end of American slavery. In 2021, Juneteenth was declared a new federal holiday.*

* A federal holiday is a holiday on which government offices are closed and government employees have the day off.

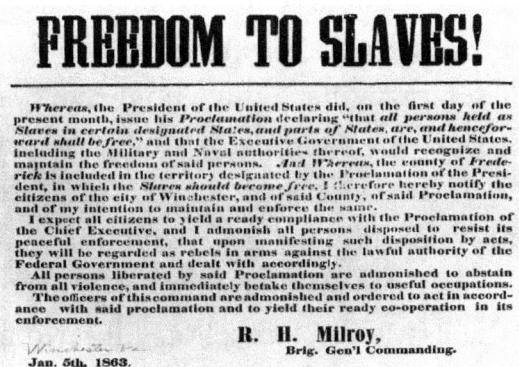

FREEDOM TO SLAVES!

Whereas, the President of the United States did, on the first day of the present month, issue his *Proclamation* declaring "that *all persons held as Slaves in certain designated States, and parts of States, are, and henceforward shall be free,*" and that the Executive Government of the United States, including the Military and Naval authorities thereof, would recognize and maintain the freedom of said persons. *And Whereas,* the county of *Frederick* is included in the territory designated by the Proclamation of the President, in which the *Slaves should become free,* I therefore hereby notify the citizens of the city of Winchester, and of said County, of said Proclamation, and of my intention to maintain and enforce the same.

I expect all citizens to yield a ready compliance with the Proclamation of the Chief Executive, and I admonish all persons disposed to resist its peaceful enforcement, that upon manifesting such disposition by acts, they will be regarded as rebels in arms against the lawful authority of the Federal Government and dealt with accordingly.

All persons liberated by said Proclamation are admonished to abstain from all violence, and immediately betake themselves to useful occupations.

The officers of this command are admonished and ordered to act in accordance with said proclamation and to yield their ready co-operation in its enforcement.

R. H. Milroy,
Brig. Gen'l Commanding.

Winchester Va.
Jan. 5th, 1863.

General Order No. 3.

The Proclamation was immediately controversial because many Northerners did not support the active abolition of slavery, preferring instead to believe (against historical evidence) that slavery would die out on its own. Nevertheless, it officially made the abolition of slavery a goal of the war, second only to the goal of reuniting the country.

First Conscription* Act (1863): This act was passed to enlist the soldiers the Union needed to continue fighting the war. It caused controversy because men who could afford to pay a $300 fee—the equivalent of about $9,500 today—were able to buy their way out of military service.

* Conscription means forcing people to enlist in the military. It can also be called "the draft," "selective service," or "induction into the military."

Battle of Gettysburg (July 1–3, 1863): This battle is generally seen as the turning point of the war. Confederate troops led by

Robert E. Lee invaded Pennsylvania, a Union state. The three-day battle that followed included **Pickett's Charge**, which occurred when Lee ordered **General Pickett** and two other Confederate generals to lead a large infantry (foot soldiers) force on a running assault that required them to run across about a mile of open field. The Confederate artillery (big guns) that was supposed to provide them with covering fire was ineffective and Union artillery killed most of the running soldiers. Those who did survive ran out of ammunition mid-battle. Historians also attribute this Confederate loss to the death of **General Thomas "Stonewall" Jackson** after the Battle of Chancellorsville two months earlier. The combined number of casualties from both armies was about 500,000.

Siege of Vicksburg (May 18–July 4, 1863): Vicksburg, Mississippi, was a valuable river transport and communication hub. **Union General Ulysses S. Grant** besieged the city for about six weeks. The North won a decisive victory that severed (cut) Confederate communications and supply routes; Confederate forces in Vicksburg surrendered on July 4, one day after the Union victory in Gettysburg.

New York Draft Riots (July 1863): White workers rioted for five days, causing thousands of injuries and deaths. They resented that men with money could buy their way out of the draft (above). They also believed that free African Americans would take their jobs while they were away fighting a war to free more black people.

The rioters were also angry that there were no African American soldiers even though their absence was entirely due to the *Dred Scott* ruling that black people were ineligible for citizenship. In response, they pressured the Lincoln administration to allow their participation. Frederick Douglass was a leader in this fight, and after the 1863 Emancipation Proclamation, President Lincoln asked him to help recruit men for new all-black army regiments and established the Bureau of Colored Troops. Ultimately, about 180,000 black soldiers served in all-black units under white officers for about half the money that white soldiers earned. There were also about 40,000 African Americans who served in the United States Navy*.

> * Black volunteers rushed to sign up when the war started. They also served in both the American Revolutionary War and the War of 1812.

Gettysburg Address (1863): Four months after the Battle of Gettysburg, Lincoln spoke at the ceremony that dedicated the battlefield as a national war monument and soldier's cemetery; 3,500 Union soldiers are buried there. The Gettysburg Address only contains 271 words, but it is extremely famous and could be used as part of a set of paired passages on SAT READING. You may even have memorized it as a school assignment. I've reproduced it here with a quick summary of the important points below.

> *Four score and seven years ago our fathers brought forth on this continent, a new nation, conceived in Liberty, and dedicated to the proposition that all men are created equal.*
>
> *Now we are engaged in a great civil war, testing whether that nation, or any nation so conceived and so dedicated, can long endure. We are met on a great battlefield of that war. We have come to dedicate a portion of that field, as a final resting place for those who here gave their lives*

that that nation might live. It is altogether fitting and proper that we should do this.

But, in a larger sense, we cannot dedicate, we cannot consecrate, we cannot hallow this ground. The brave men, living and dead, who struggled here, have consecrated it, far above our poor power to add or detract. The world will little note, nor long remember what we say here, but it can never forget what they did here. It is for us the living, rather, to be dedicated here to the unfinished work which they who fought here have thus far so nobly advanced. It is rather for us to be here dedicated to the great task remaining before us— that from these honored dead we take increased devotion to that cause for which they gave the last full measure of devotion—that we here highly resolve that these dead shall not have died in vain—that this nation, under God, shall have a new birth of freedom— and that government of the people, by the people, for the people, shall not perish from the earth.

A "score" of years is twenty years, so "fourscore and seven years" is eighty-seven years, the number of years between 1776 and 1867. Lincoln says that eighty-seven years ago, the United States was founded on the ideals of liberty and human equality and that it is appropriate to create a cemetery to honor soldiers who died to keep the country unified. He goes on to say that the ceremony they are having to consecrate (make holy) the battlefield will be forgotten but that the "honored dead" will always be remembered as long as the North keeps fighting to ensure that the United States' "government of the people, by the people, and for the people" will last forever.

Sherman's March (1863–1864): In April 1864, Northern forces led by Union **General William Tecumseh Sherman** entered Atlanta, Georgia, and burned about 40 percent of it, including its industrial district and anything that the Confederate Army might be able to use. Sherman then led his troops on an indirect 250-mile march across Georgia from Atlanta to Savannah, an important Confederate seaport and supply depot. Sherman's army deliberately burned, stole, and destroyed anything that could be of use to the Confederacy. Union soldiers were under orders to supply themselves by taking food from Confederate supply depots and private citizens as they marched. The railroad tracks that they melted down and twisted became known as "Sherman's neckties."

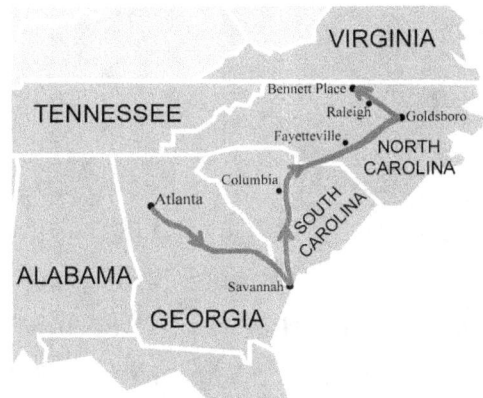

Sherman's March.

General Sherman's successful campaign helped President Lincoln win reelection in 1864. The Confederacy began to fall apart because it lacked men, food to feed them, and supplies for them to continue fighting. Much of the South's infrastructure had been destroyed, and Confederate soldiers began deserting because they were hungry and hadn't been paid.

President Lincoln was reelected in November 1864, and his second **Inaugural Address** has appeared as an SAT READING Passage. It focuses on the need to heal the divided country. He says that the Civil War is God's punishment on the country for the sin of slavery and that ending slavery will atone (make up) for that sin.

Confederate Army Surrenders: On April 9, 1865, Confederate General Robert E. Lee formally surrendered to Union General Ulysses S. Grant, bringing the Civil War to an end. In just four years, nearly 650,000 men had died, a number that represents almost half of all American dead in all the wars the United States has fought to date. The South had more war deaths per capita (per person*) than the North did because its smaller white population meant that a greater percentage of white men fought and died in the South.

* |Per white person.

The landscape of the South was also destroyed. The four-year **Union Blockade** had starved the Confederacy of trade and supplies, and Sherman's March and similar campaigns had destroyed railroad tracks, bridges, and other infrastructure. The abolition of slavery meant that there was no labor force. Fields lay fallow (unplanted) or were burned, and people who used Confederate money found that it was suddenly worthless.

Lincoln's Assassination: Two days after the Confederacy surrendered, President Lincoln introduced the idea of "reconstructing" the nation as a unified, prosperous whole. He proposed working with the former Confederate states to help them rebuild. He said that white Southerners should be given time to adjust to being "free States" and that they should be warmly welcomed back into the Union. He also said that he would support giving the vote to "very intelligent" African American men and to "those who serve our cause as soldiers."

Today, many people would be offended because Lincoln's support for letting "very intelligent" black men vote implies that not all black people are smart enough to vote. At the time, however, his suggestion infuriated **John Wilkes Booth**, who supposedly declared that Lincoln had just made his final speech. Three days later, on April 15, 1865, Booth shot Lincoln at close range while he was watching a play at Ford's Theater in Washington, DC. After twelve days on the run, Booth was captured and killed. Booth had conspirators who were supposed to assassinate other government officials, but they failed to kill their targets and were eventually tried and hanged for treason.

United States (1865–1914)

History is always complex and messy, and the period between the end of the Civil War and the end of the nineteenth century is no exception. In addition to the rise and fall of **Reconstruction** and the development of race-based segregation as the law of the South, this period includes the **Second Industrial Revolution**, the **Gilded Age** and the **Progressive Era** as well as the **Women's Rights** and **Labor** movements. These different terms for the same thirty-five-year period are a great reminder that all of this was happening at the same time. SAT READING and SAT WRITING both frequently include passages from or about this period.

Reconstruction (1865–1877): After the Civil War ended, the Union government wanted to reintegrate the Southern states that had seceded. It also wanted to help formerly enslaved people to build successful lives by building schools, increasing literacy and participating in politics. Over fifty all-black towns were established, as well as many all-black colleges and universities. Black people eagerly entered into the life of the nation, opening businesses and running for political office.

Forty Acres and a Mule: After meeting with leaders of the newly emancipated African American community, General Sherman issued "Special Field Orders No. 15," in which he decreed that 400,000 acres of Georgia, South Carolina, and Florida that his army had captured in battles with the Confederacy would be set aside—in parcels of up to 40 acres—exclusively for black ownership and governance. Later, Sherman added a provision that said the United States Army could loan mules to these new landowners.

President Andrew Johnson: President Lincoln's first vice president, Hannibal Hamlin, was a member of the anti-slavery Republican* party. When Lincoln decided to run for reelection, he decided to replace Hamlin with **Andrew Johnson**, one of the few slaveholding Southerners who remained loyal to the Union after the Southern states seceded.

> * In the nineteenth century, the Republican Party
> was liberal and abolitionist, whereas the Democratic
> Party was conservative and pro-slavery. This
> remained true until the 1960s, when the Democratic
> Party supported the Civil Rights Movement, and the
> Republicans, in general, did not.

After Lincoln's assassination, Johnson resisted calls from Republicans to deal harshly with the former Confederacy and initially seemed to support Lincoln's plan to avoid punishing the defeated Confederate states. However, he opposed ending slavery and pardoned many Confederate leaders and military officials. He returned the land that had been allocated (set aside) for the newly freed by Special Field Orders No. 15 to its original slave-holding owners and tried to veto the **Thirteenth Amendment**.

Thirteenth Amendment: Passed in early 1865, the Thirteenth Amendment to the Constitution says that no one in the United States can be forced into slavery or involuntary servitude (forced labor) except as a punishment for a crime. Although the Thirteenth Amendment was intended to end slavery in the United States, this loophole—"except as punishment for a crime"—made it possible for white Southerners to create new crimes that they included in **Black Codes** (laws designed to enforce racial segregation and create slavery-like conditions for black people). For example, Mississippi passed a law that said black people had to pay a fine if they didn't have a year's work lined up in advance on New Year's Day. Another tactic was to arrest black men for minor crimes like loitering (standing around in public). Judges handed out long sentences that included hard labor, essentially recreating slavery.

Incarcerated black children were required to work in the fields.

The Fourteenth Amendment says that anyone born in the United States is a citizen (birthright citizenship), free and equal to all other citizens. It also guarantees all citizens "equal protection under the law."

The Fifteenth Amendment builds on the Fourteenth Amendment, saying that no (male) citizen's right to vote can be taken away by either the federal government or any state as a result of "race, color or previous condition of servitude." However, between 1890 and 1910, all eleven former Confederate states enacted laws that either circumvented (worked around) or simply ignored federal law. These state laws included poll taxes—fees for the privilege of voting—that most blacks and some whites were too poor to afford. Other laws required black people to pass difficult literacy tests that no white people ever had to take and that were designed to be impossible to pass. Finally, white supremacist militias such as the **Ku Klux Klan (KKK)** threatened, beat, or murdered black men who tried to vote. As a result, African Americans remained disenfranchised (unable to vote) throughout the South until the passage of the Voting Rights Act six decades later.

By 1910, virtually every Southern state had passed comprehensive Black Codes that effectively segregated people by race and made sure that black people always got the worst of every situation. This system of segregation (separation) of people by race is often referred to as "**Jim Crow.**" The name "Jim Crow" is attributed (credited) to a song called "Jump Jim Crow" that was part of a white performer's act that was performed in blackface makeup to caricature (mock) supposedly stereotypical black behavior.

Sharecropping: After the war, many former slaveholders divided their plantations into small plots that they rented to former slaves and poor whites. Like serfs, sharecroppers were obligated (required) to raise cash crops—rice, cotton, or tobacco—and to give a portion to the landowner. In addition to providing housing and land to sharecropping farmers, owners often acted like banks for their tenants, loaning them money for seed and other farm supplies in the spring and charging them interest on top of the amount they borrowed. This system worked well in terms of raising cash crops and bringing them to market, but it also left sharecroppers at the mercy of unscrupulous (dishonest) landlords who could charge high interest rates for loans and set exorbitant (outrageously high) prices for things their tenants needed. All this was in addition to the portion of the crop that the tenant owed the owner.

Plessy v. Ferguson (1896): This Supreme Court decision upheld Black Codes and racial segregation by saying that it was okay to segregate people by race as long as they had equal treatment in their separate groups. Although this might have sounded good in theory, in practice the doctrine of "separate but equal" generally meant that facilities for whites were better than those for blacks and that they could be legally excluded from all-white institutions and professions.

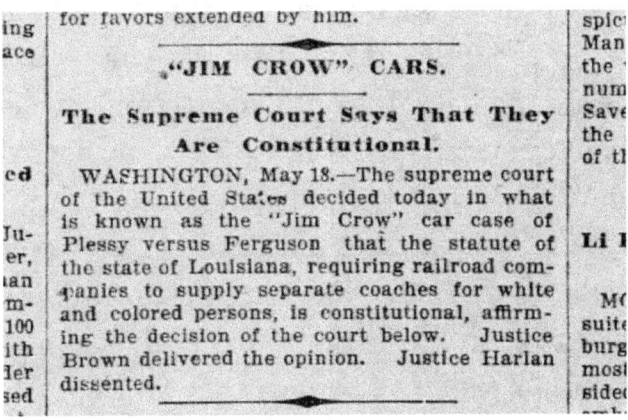

A newspaper report on *Plessy v. Ferguson*.

Immigration: Twelve million immigrants, mostly from Europe, arrived on the shores of the United States between 1865 and 1900, including about one million from China. At first, the vast majority were German, English, or Irish; this was no different from how it had always been. In the 1870s, however, more people from southern and eastern Europe began to arrive. The new arrivals were thrust into the middle of a rapidly growing, changing society and participated in all of the movements and events that were taking place in the United States.

Most immigrants arriving from Europe went through **Ellis Island*** in New York. They lived primarily in major cities such as Boston, New York, Philadelphia, Chicago, and St. Louis. Cities grew rapidly, and by 1900, about 40 percent of all Americans lived in cities. This rapid growth, combined with the arrival of often penniless immigrants, led to the creation of dirty, overcrowded tenements (slum-like apartments). People worked as many as one hundred hours a week, and workers had no protections against poor treatment, wage cuts, or unemployment.

* | The Ellis Island Immigration Center.

As a result of the 1845 Irish potato famine (above), Irish immigrants made up about one-third of all immigrants to the United States in the second half of the nineteenth century. They arrived malnourished (underfed) and often ill from the harsh conditions they had suffered in Ireland and during the Atlantic crossing. They settled in east coast cities like Boston, New York, and Philadelphia, cities that had been founded centuries earlier by Protestants fleeing Catholic oppression. Anti-Catholic, anti-Irish sentiment was strong, fueled by rumors that the Pope was planning a Catholic takeover of the United States and that Catholic priests and nuns were sexual deviants who murdered babies.

Irish immigrants were largely unskilled, so they worked at the most undesirable, lowest-paid jobs. Political and editorial cartoons depicted them with simian (ape-like) facial features, compared them to people of African descent and routinely denied them employment.

> WANTED—A good, reliable woman to take the care of a boy two years old, in a small family in Brookline. Good wages and a permanent situation given. No washing or ironing will be required, but good recommendations as to character and capacity demanded. Positively no Irish need apply. Call at 24 Washington street, corner of Summer street.
> ut   Jy 2s

Religious discrimination put new Irish immigrants
at the bottom of the social scale.

Chinese Exclusion Act (1882): Beginning in the 1850s, a steadily growing stream of Chinese immigrants began arriving in California and Oregon, often entering through the immigrant processing center on **Angel Island** in San Francisco. Many were men who hoped to send money to desperate families back in China. They mined for gold during the **California Gold Rush**, built large portions of the Transcontinental Railroad, and worked in farming and the garment industry. Their willingness to work for extremely low wages angered poor whites who feared the Chinese would take their jobs. California passed a number of anti-Chinese laws, including one that said they could not testify in court against white people. Chinese immigrants were frequently subjected to humiliation, violence, and even murder. White people often refused to use Chinese-owned businesses and sometimes set them on fire. In 1875, the **Page Act** banned Chinese women from immigrating to the United States, and in 1882, the **Chinese Exclusion Act** banned all Chinese immigration.

This poster characterizes anti-Chinese sentiment as all-American.

Women's Rights: Women were second-class citizens in nineteenth-century America. They could not vote, attend college, enter most professions, testify in court, or serve on juries. When a woman married, her property became her husband's, and if she worked, he could keep her wages for himself. Husbands had the right to beat and imprison their wives. It was not legally possible for a man to rape his wife—even if he injured her—because husbands were entitled to sex on demand. In cases of divorce, husbands routinely gained custody of all but the youngest children.

In 1848, the **Seneca Falls Convention** was held in Seneca Falls, New York. It was the first event that women had ever organized to discuss their own status in society. Although Frederick Douglass was one of the speakers, men were only permitted to attend on the second day. The **"Declaration of Sentiments"** revises the language of the Declaration of Independence to include both sexes: "We hold these truths to be self-evident; that all men *and* *women** are created equal." The "Declaration of Sentiments" has been used for SAT READING passages, as has Douglass's speech and those of the convention's organizers, **Elizabeth Cady Stanton** and **Lucretia Mott**.

* | Italics indicate my emphasis.

At the 1851 Women's Convention in Akron, Ohio, the formerly enslaved abolitionist and feminist preacher **Sojourner Truth** responded to a man's claim that women were too dainty and weak to withstand the rough-and-tumble of the public world of men by giving her famous "Ain't I a Woman" speech. In it, she says that she worked as hard as any man while enslaved—while also bearing thirteen children, only to see most of them sold away from her.

Suffrage (the right to vote) advocate **Susan B. Anthony** was arrested, tried, and convicted of voting illegally in the 1872 presidential election, and the speech she gave at her trial, **"On Women's Right to Vote,"** has been used as an SAT READING passage. In it, Anthony uses the arguments of earlier feminists to explain how women in the United States have been systematically deprived of the rights that are guaranteed by the United States Constitution.

At first, the women's rights movement included both white and African American women. However, the debate surrounding the 1870 passage of the Fifteenth Amendment, which gave black men the right to vote, revealed the racism of many white feminists. For example, when white feminists Elizabeth Cady Stanton and Susan B. Anthony wrote their 1881 book, *History of Woman Suffrage*, they did not include the contributions of black women. They also refused to allow black women to join the **National Woman Suffrage Association** or attend its conventions.

African American women responded to the racism of white feminists and the sexism of the Fifteenth Amendment* by founding their own organizations. Many prioritized the struggle for African American rights because they felt that racism was a bigger problem than sexism in their lives. Many African American feminists—such as Harriet Tubman, Sojourner Truth, **Mary Church Terrell**, and **Frances Ellen Watkins Harper**—were eloquent writers and speakers whose work could be used for SAT READING.

> * Only black men could vote. Black women were excluded because of their gender.

Second Industrial Revolution: The **Transcontinental Railroad,** completed in 1869, connected the eastern United States to San Francisco and the Pacific coast. The telegraph and, starting in 1876, the telephone, made it possible to communicate quickly and cheaply over long distances. Typewriters, carpet sweepers, bicycles, elevators, cash registers, photography, internal combustion engines, barbed wire, light bulbs, dynamite, and mail order catalogs are among the many inventions that made life faster, cheaper, and more efficient. SAT WRITING can include passages about the benefits or unintended negative consequences of a new invention or a proposal to solve the problems of urban overcrowding and poor living conditions.

the sweeper with
the self-cleaning brush
OF PURE BRISTLE
THE UNIQUE
FLEETWAY
"SWIFT"

Every machine precision-built.
One-piece delightfully stream-
lined metal case · rubber-
tyred wheels · automatic
dust-pan action · attractively
finished in daffodil, turquoise,
red or black.   37/9
From Furnishing and Hardware Stores.   Tax paid.
FLEETWAY MANUFACTURING CO. LTD.
WINTON HOUSE, ST. ANDREW ST., LONDON, E.C.4

Carpet sweepers are mechanical rug-cleaning devices that
were popular before the invention of electric vacuum cleaners.

Gilded Age (1870–1900): The "Gilded Age" takes its name from a novel by American author **Mark Twain** whose work is often excerpted by SAT READING. It refers to the luxurious lifestyles of the very wealthy and suggests that shiny surfaces hide ugly realities. In other words, the Gilded Age was a time of great progress and wealth, but it was also a time of steep income inequality, corruption, and injustice.

Businessmen such as **Andrew Carnegie, Cornelius Vanderbilt,** and **J.D. Rockefeller,** known as "**Captains of Industry,**" monopolized (completely controlled) entire industries and accumulated vast personal wealth, and their writing on topics such as the federal income tax has appeared on SAT READING. You might also see paired passages arguing about the causes of poverty or whether the rich should give to the poor.

Progressive Era (1890s–1920s): The Progressive Era arose in response to enormous social turmoil (disruption). About twenty million people arrived in the United States, mostly from Europe, increasing the population by about 60 percent in forty years.

Urban immigrants, many of whom arrived penniless, clustered in cities where they interacted with rural Americans drawn by the promise of manufacturing jobs. In the South, the end of Reconstruction allowed Black Codes to become law, and many African Americans lived in poverty and struggled to survive in a system that was designed to make them fail.

Solutions to Urban Poverty: The profession of **social work** developed from centuries-old traditions of giving charity to the poor and claimed to be a "scientific" approach to solving poverty. British social reformer **Octavia Hill** is considered the profession's founder, and her work was influenced by the economic and philosophical ideas of her time. In 1869, she wrote, "Where a man persistently refuses to exert himself, external help is worse than useless." This essay was influenced by **Ralph Waldo Emerson's** 1841 essay **"Self-Reliance"** from which SAT READING has taken multiple passages.

By the 1880s, cities in both England and the United States were overrun with poor workers who could not afford housing. The **Settlement House** movement worked to alleviate (lessen) both homelessness and social class differences by providing large housing projects that were affordable and open to all. In the United States, **Jane Addams** and **Ellen Gates Starr** founded **Hull House** in Chicago, and its campus grew to include several buildings, children's housing, playgrounds, a gymnasium, and stores. Starr and Addams also advocated for child labor laws, the establishment of children's protection agencies, and the juvenile court system. They also supported workers' rights and women's right to vote. Addams was a prolific (productive) writer, and excerpts from her work have appeared on SAT READING.

Muckraking: Newspaper reporters known as **muckrakers** exposed political corruption and profiteering (making unfair profits). Political cartoonist Thomas Nast waged a successful campaign against **William Magear "Boss" Tweed**, the head of the New York Democratic Party in New York City, by depicting him as a bloated capitalist and his administration as vultures waiting to feast on the carcasses of the poor. Public opinion turned against Tweed, and he was later jailed for stealing at least twenty-five million dollars of public money for his own benefit.

Muckrakers also reported on injustice and the mistreatment of the poor and vulnerable, and their writings have appeared on SAT READING. They documented urban poverty, unhygienic (unhealthy) working conditions, and the harmful effects of child labor. **Florence Kelley's** reporting on poor women and children led to shorter work shifts—only ten hours a day instead of twelve or fourteen—and public funding for women's and children's health. **Jacob Riis** photographed the squalid (poor and dirty) living conditions in the slums of New York, Philadelphia, and Boston. The outrage his photographs caused led to new city housing for the poor. **Nellie Bly**, one of the earliest investigative journalists, pretended to be insane and went undercover as a patient in an insane asylum for ten days; her reporting led the asylum to reform its practices. **Upton Sinclair's** 1906 novel, *The Jungle*, targeted unhygienic practices in the meat and dairy industries and led to the creation of the **United States Food and Drug Administration.**

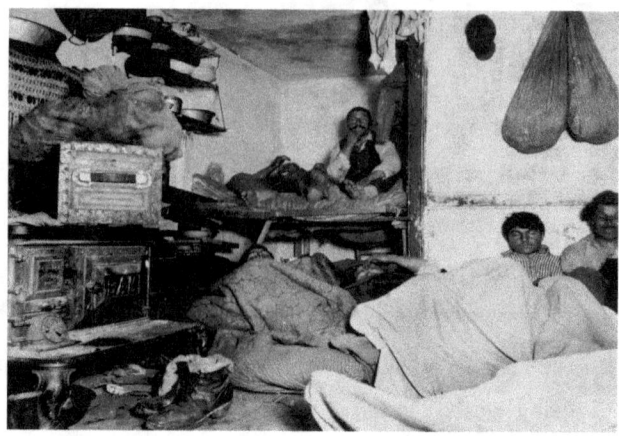

An immigrant family in the slums, photographed by Jacob Riis.

African American Progressives: African Americans found themselves unwelcome among white progressives, so they formed their own organizations and worked to improve conditions within black communities. For example, **Ida B. Wells** wrote and spoke about white mob violence and frequent lynching (when someone is hanged by a mob) of African Americans at a time when such crimes against African Americans occurred frequently and openly.

However, African American leaders of the time did not all agree with each other about the best way to secure equal rights for black people. **W. E. B. Du Bois** (pronounced *doo-BOIZ*) and **Booker T. Washington** shared the same goals but disagreed on the best way to achieve them. Du Bois was the first African American to earn a PhD from Harvard, and he did important research on slavery and the postwar lives of Southern blacks for the American government in the 1890s. He also advocated for equal rights and an end to the "color line" (segregation) in his book, *The Souls of Black Folk.* The book includes an essay that he wrote after his young son died from diphtheria because no white doctor in Atlanta, Georgia, would treat him.

The Souls of Black Folk also includes Du Bois's famous work on **double consciousness**—the idea that for their own safety, black people must constantly think about how white people will perceive them. He promoted the idea of the **Talented Tenth**, an argument that the most educated African Americans, roughly one in ten, would lead the remaining 90 percent to equality. Eventually, he became a communist and left the United States to spend his remaining years in Ghana. His legacy as a communist tarnished his reputation as a prominent African American leader because communists were viewed as hostile to American democracy (below).

Booker T. Washington was born into slavery. He was the founder of the historically black Tuskegee University, adviser to several American presidents, and the most prominent African American leader of his time. He was a staunch (firm) supporter of African American-owned businesses. He counseled black people to be patient and to focus on improving their lot through education and hard work instead of working to overturn segregation and voter suppression in court. Both Washington and Du Bois have been used for SAT READING. It's possible you will see paired passages in which they disagree completely or partially with each other.

Marcus Garvey: In the early twentieth century, Jamaican-born **Marcus Garvey** became convinced that people of African descent in the United States, Jamaica, and other Caribbean islands would never be able to live freely until they gained political autonomy (independence). Garvey settled in New York City, where he founded the **Universal Negro Improvement Association (UNIA)** to promote racial pride and support African American businesses.

In 1919, Garvey founded a company dedicated to transporting African Americans back to Africa. His work attracted thousands of followers, who dubbed him the "Black Moses." In 1920, he rented a large hall, where he delivered his "Declaration of the Rights of the Negro Peoples of the World" before a crowd of 25,000. Like any manifesto of rights, it could be used for SAT READING.

Temperance* Movement: Europeans and North Americans were accustomed to drinking low-alcohol beer or watered-down wine throughout the day. These beverages provided nutrition and calories, and the alcohol helped prevent sickness by killing bacteria in the water.

> * | Abstaining from alcoholic beverages.

Nineteenth-century American farmers produced more corn than they could transport to cities for sale as food, so they began to make it into whiskey, which has a much higher alcohol content than wine or beer. It was plentiful and cheap, so people drank it throughout the day, even while at work. Alcoholism—then called drunkenness—became a public health concern, although it was considered a moral problem rather than a disease*. Violence rose, especially domestic violence. The **Temperance Movement** began by telling people to moderate their alcohol intake, but the movement soon fractured because some activists wanted to ban alcohol altogether.

> * | The American Medical Association first labeled alcoholism a disease in 1956.

During the Progressive Era, the Temperance Movement gained nationwide support. Alcohol consumption was blamed for poverty, child neglect and domestic abuse. Many women joined the movement from feminist motivations—in a culture that did not provide women and children with protection from domestic abuse, preventing men from drinking seemed like the best way to protect vulnerable (at risk) women and children.

There were a number of all-women temperance groups during the Progressive Era.

The Labor Movement: The immigration of millions of people often meant that there were more people who wanted work than there were jobs to employ them. This worker surplus meant that the "Captains of Industry," who made great fortunes during the Gilded Age, had no incentive (reason) to pay their workers well or to provide them with safe working conditions. Any worker who complained could be replaced, sometimes for even less pay.

Trade unions predate the American Revolutionary War, but the influx of millions of immigrants in search of better lives energized the labor movement. Many of them believed that capitalism is an inherently (naturally) unjust system and that only a communist, socialist, or anarchist* revolution would bring justice to exploited workers. The Chicago Haymarket Riot (1886) occurred during a large rally organized by anarchists to protest the police killings of several strikers. When police arrived, someone threw a bomb, and the police and some rally attendees exchanged fire. Many people were injured or killed, including seven police officers. In response, the anarchist leaders were arrested, and four of them were ultimately executed for their role in the fighting.

✳ Anarchists believe that all government authority is bad.

Coverage of the Haymarket Square Riot

Pinkerton Detective Agency: In the 1850s, Scottish immigrant **Allan Pinkerton** founded the **Pinkerton Detective Agency**. He provided security for President Lincoln during the Civil War and hired women and racial minorities at a time when most white employers refused to do so. After the war, the agency was often hired to break workers' strikes and safeguard new workers hired to replace strikers. Pinkerton detectives became notorious for violent methods that often resulted in strikers' injuries and deaths.

The **Homestead Strike** (1892) occurred when steel magnate (industry leader) Andrew Carnegie increased the hours and lowered the wages of workers in his steel mill in Homestead, Pennsylvania. The workers protested by going on strike, so Carnegie ordered his plant manager to lock them out. He sent three hundred armed Pinkerton detectives against ten thousand strikers, many of whom were also armed. After a day-long battle that left sixteen people dead, the detectives surrendered. Carnegie then convinced the Pennsylvania governor to send eight thousand militia (citizen soldiers) against the strikers. The union lost, Carnegie Steel imposed longer hours and lower pay for workers, and the Pinkerton detectives were honored by having a Chicago bridge named after them.

Pullman Strike (1893): The Pullman Palace Car Company of Chicago, Illinois, built railroad cars. It responded to an economic slump by cutting workers' pay by 25 percent. When the workers went on strike and shut down large portions of the country's rail network, the company locked them out of the factory. Violence broke out and a United States mail train was derailed by strikers, so President Grover Cleveland sent federal troops to Chicago to protect the mail. More violence ensued (followed), people died, and everyone came out poorer.

Company owner George Pullman is portrayed as a fat capitalist committed to wringing every penny out of his workers while refusing to cut rent and other fees in his company town.

Triangle Shirtwaist* Factory Fire (1911): The owners of the Triangle Shirtwaist Factory in New York City were notoriously hostile to workers' rights. The factory was on the eighth, ninth, and tenth floors of the building and it employed young immigrant women to work twelve-hour shifts seven days a week. Exit doors were kept locked from the outside to prevent workers from taking bathroom breaks. When the fire broke out, hundreds of women were trapped in the building. Many leapt to their deaths and firefighters found bodies piled six feet deep when they finally opened the locked doors that had prevented the women from escaping. Despite 146 deaths and extreme public outrage, the factory owners were acquitted (found not guilty) of any wrongdoing and only paid each deceased worker's family a small amount. However, the tragedy did result in significantly stronger fire prevention laws in New York City.

> * A shirtwaist is a woman's blouse and can either be a separate garment or attached to a skirt to create a dress.

Spanish-American War (April–August 1898): At the end of the nineteenth century, the United States used the Monroe Doctrine (above) to justify American support for Cuban independence from Spain in the **Spanish-American War**. Americans sympathized with the Cuban rebels, who reminded them of their own struggle against the colonial British—especially when they read sensationalized (overly dramatic) newspaper accounts of how badly the Spanish were treating the Cuban rebels. Future United States president **Theodore Roosevelt** resigned as the Secretary of the Navy and formed the "**Rough Riders**," a volunteer cavalry (soldiers on horseback) unit that became famous for winning the **Battle of San Juan Hill**. There was also fighting in the Philippines, where the United States again drove Spain out and took control. After the war ended, Cuba was independent and the United States gained Puerto Rico, the Philippines, and the Mariana Islands as territories. Puerto Rico and the Mariana Islands are still United States territories, but the Philippines became an independent nation in 1946.

World War I (1914–1918)

World War I is also known as the "Great War," especially before World War II, which of course was an even "greater" war because even more countries were involved and many more people died. At the time, people also called World War I **"The War to End All Wars"** because they believed that ending military conflict was possible. The Progressive Era was still in full swing and people were idealistic about the future. Many believed that human progress would continue indefinitely and that all the world's problems were going to be solved soon.

European Geopolitics: The map of 1914 Europe was different from the one that exists today. The borders of Spain, France, Italy, and Portugal are much the same as they were at the beginning of World War I, but the German Empire's former territory is now the independent countries of Germany and Poland. Turkey has replaced the Ottoman Empire. The large territory formerly controlled by the Austro-Hungarian Empire is now divided into the Balkans*.

> * The Balkans include Albania, Bosnia, Croatia, the Czech Republic, Herzegovina, Hungary, Macedonia, Moldova, Serbia, Slovakia, and Slovenia.

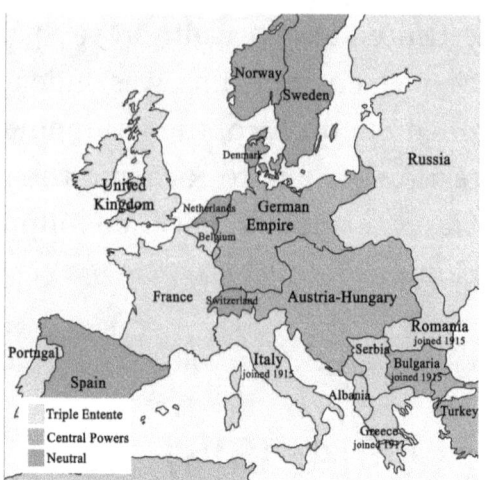

A map of Europe as it was in 1914. The Triple Entente
was another name for the Allied Powers.

The European peace established in 1815 at the Congress of
Vienna (above) was still in place, but Europeans themselves were
more divided. Each country maintained a standing army in case
it was attacked as well as a network of secret mutual (shared)
defense treaties in which each party promised to aid the others
if they were attacked. Finally, nationalist movements developed,
most notably in the Austro-Hungarian Empire. When the empire
annexed Bosnia and Herzegovina in 1908, Bosnians and Herzego-
vinians were not happy about this loss of independence. Revolutionary groups planned and schemed to free their countries
from the empire.

Assassination of Archduke Franz Ferdinand: On June 28, 1914,
Archduke Franz Ferdinand, the heir to the throne of the Austro-Hungarian Empire, toured Sarajevo, the capital of Bosnia
and Herzegovina, with no security whatsoever*. Seated in an
open car, he took a slow, stately ride down a major thorough-
fare lined with crowds of people, so it was easy for a revolutionary, **Gavrilo Princip,** to assassinate him. Princip went to jail for

murdering the archduke, but the assassination set off a chain of events that led to the start of the deadliest war in human history (again, until World War II) with about twenty-two million deaths and another twenty-one million wounded.

* | This was not particularly unusual at the time.

War Begins: The beginning of the war included a lot of complicated geopolitical maneuvering as all the secret mutual defense treaties kicked in, but you don't really need to know most of it for the SAT. You should, however, understand the broad outlines of the conflict and how it affected the course of the twentieth century. You should also know that World War I marked the first time airplanes, flamethrowers and tanks were used in war and that this increased mechanization of warfare contributed to the war's high number of casualties. The single bloodiest day of the war occurred on July 1, 1916, at the Battle of the Somme: one million casualties, including three hundred thousand deaths.

The **Central Powers** included the German Empire, the Austro-Hungarian Empire, the Ottoman Empire, and Bulgaria. They are also called the "**Triple Alliance**." The **Allied Powers** were France, Russia, Great Britain, Romania, Japan, Italy, and (in 1917) the United States. Italy switched sides partway through the war and Japan's poor treatment by the other victorious Allied nations at the end of the war caused it to ally itself with Germany against the Allies in World War II.

When the war began in 1914, many British and German soldiers believed the fighting would last about three months and that they would all be home by Christmas. Young British men, raised on romanticized stories of the Boer Wars (above), rushed to volunteer. Many Germans believed that their army was invincible (could not be defeated).

The German army committed itself to fighting Russia on its "**eastern front**" (eastern border) and England and France on its "**western front.**" However, it badly underestimated the military capabilities of the French and British, and the war quickly became a prolonged stalemate. Hundreds of miles of trenches (ditches) and barbed wire soon lined the western front and both armies were more or less stuck in place. Despite this lack of movement, improvements in the aim and distance of long-range artillery allowed the armies to inflict horrifying casualties on each other. The German army began firing canisters of poisonous gas at British and French troops, causing terrible injuries and terrifying Allied soldiers.

Submarine Warfare: The submarine was invented in the early seventeenth century (1600s) and first used in warfare during the American Revolutionary War. In World War I, the Germans added submarines to their fleet of warships. After the war began, they used submarines against non-military ships because they knew that the British and their allies used them to transport weapons. In total, they sank about five thousand non-military ships. They did try, however, to avoid civilian casualties from neutral countries such as the United States.

Sinking of the *Lusitania* (1915): The Germans planned to attack the *Lusitania*, an ocean liner (large, luxurious passenger ship), but they did not want to cause civilian casualties. Far in advance of the *Lusitania's* sailing, the Germans placed newspaper advertisements that warned people against booking passage (buying tickets) on it. However, the ads did not prevent about 1,200 passengers, including 128 Americans, from setting sail, and the *Lusitania's* sinking helped to draw the United States into World War I. The large number of civilian casualties was widely condemned as a war crime in both England and the United States.

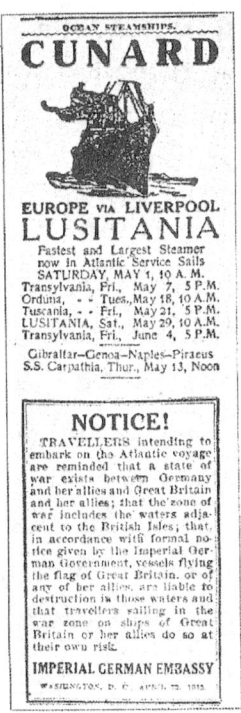

The Germans tried to warn Americans
against sailing on the *Lusitania*.

Zimmerman Telegram (1917): At first, the United States remained on the sidelines of World War I. The Germans did not want America to help the Allied Powers, even in non-military ways, so they tried to create distractions that would turn the United States' attention away from Europe. They offered financial and military support to Mexico if it would invade the United States and promised that Mexico could reclaim the territory it had lost to the United States in the Mexican-American War (above).

German Foreign Minister **Arthur Zimmerman** sent an encoded telegram to the Mexicans offering a military alliance with Germany if the United States entered the war. However, the telegram was intercepted and decoded by British cryptographers (code breakers). Its publication heightened (increased) tensions between Germany and the United States and made it more difficult for **President Woodrow Wilson** to withstand pressure to go to war. The Mexicans declined to ally with Germany, and America declared war on Germany on April 6, 1917.

Not all Americans supported President Wilson's declaration of war. Some were strong isolationists who believed America's two oceans protected it. They thought the United States should stick to the Monroe Doctrine (above) and stay out of "foreign wars." Others were pacifists who opposed all war on principle, and still others agreed with communist and socialist interpretations that viewed the war as a capitalist ploy (trick) to get the poor and powerless to fight for a cause that would only benefit the rich. Then, as now, war was complicated and controversial.

When the United States did finally join the war, it instituted a draft (forced registration for military service) through the **Selective Service Act** of 1917*. Although many young Americans signed up to fight enthusiastically (and even lied about their age to do it), the draft was deeply unpopular in parts of the American

Midwest. The **Green Corn Rebellion** was a (failed) socialist uprising of Oklahoma farmers who believed that going to war would
leave their families short of labor and vulnerable to bankruptcy
and loss of their farms. About six thousand Germans who lived
in the United States were interned (imprisoned) to prevent them
from helping the German war effort. Excerpts from speeches by
those opposed to the war, the draft, and the harsh suppression
of anti-war voices in the press have appeared as SAT READING
passages.

> * "Selective service" means using a lottery to *select*
> (draft) men from a list of eligible adult men.

President Wilson was in office from 1913–1921. When the United
States entered the war, he included the need "to make the world
safe for democracy" among his reasons. SAT READING has included
excerpts from his **"Fourteen Points"** speech of 1918, in which
he laid out a model for world politics based on transparency and
trust. Wilson also proposed the creation of a **League of Nations**,
an international organization that could mediate (help settle)
disputes among nations and avoid another European war*. He
also established the **Federal Reserve**, which regulates banking,
and the **Federal Trade Commission**, which investigates and prohibits unfair business practices, so it's possible that a speech on
one of these topics could be used as well, possibly in a set of
paired passages.

> * The United States refused to join the League of
> Nations despite President Wilson's support for it.
> The organization disbanded after failing to prevent
> World War II.

It's also conceivable (possible) that you could see an SAT WRITING passage about Wilson's views on race in America because he was not a supporter of racial equality. In fact, he supported racial segregation and passed a law forbidding interracial marriage in Washington, DC, shortly after taking office in 1913. He also required all applicants for federal jobs to attach photographs to their applications and expelled a civil rights activist from the White House.

Women in Wartime: About four million American men served in the military during World War I. Their absence from home caused labor shortages that gave women the opportunity to work in jobs that had previously been filled by men. For example, when the United States Navy needed more sailors in combat, it became the first branch of the United States military to enlist women in non-combat positions. During the war, both at home and overseas, women worked as machine operators, truck drivers, medical personnel, translators, and telephone operators—all jobs that had previously been filled by men.

Treaty of Versailles: Once the United States entered the war, Germany was outmanned and outgunned. On November 11, 1918, it surrendered to the Allies. In 1919, leaders from both sides of the conflict convened (got together) at the Palace of Versailles in France to hash out the details of Germany's surrender. The Allies blamed Germany for starting the war by invading Belgium, so they limited the size of its military to only 100,000 soldiers and six battleships. They wanted Germany to pay for the lives lost and damage done, so the peace treaty included large reparations (payments) that the Germans were required to pay in large installments. In addition to monetary (financial) reparations, the Allies also claimed all of Germany's colonies and returned the territory that Germany had won in the war to its original owners.

The European allies and the United States disregarded Japan's contributions to the Allied war effort when they omitted language about racial equality from the treaty. The Japanese felt angry and humiliated. Anti-Asian prejudice in the United States and Europe was strong and contributed to the Japanese decision to fight on Germany's side during World War II.

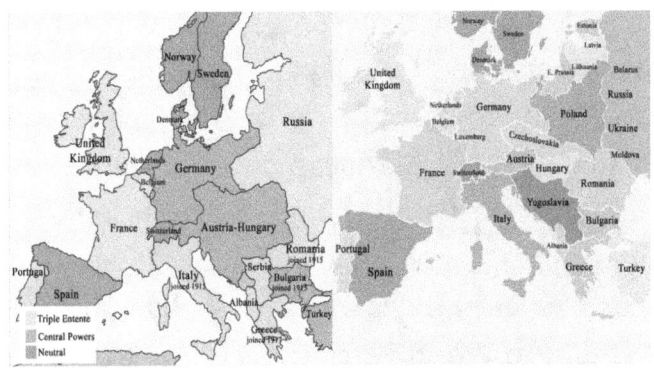

Europe before and after World War I.

The victorious Allies redrew the maps of Europe and the Middle East. Three empires—German, Ottoman, and Austro-Hungarian—had collapsed or been destroyed, and the Allies replaced them with a number of small, independent countries instead. However, they drew the national boundaries of these countries without considering whether the people within those boundaries regarded themselves as a group.

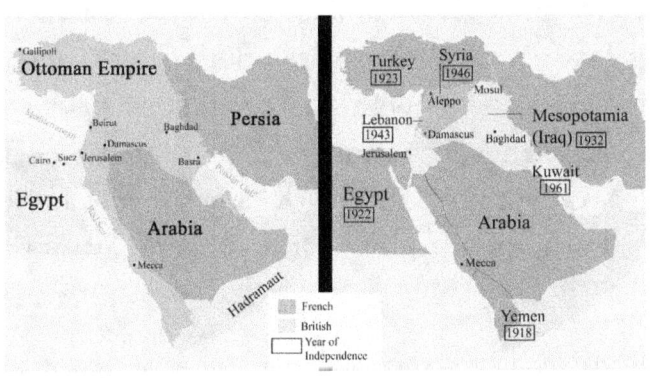

1914   The Middle East   1918

Similarly, the end of the Ottoman Empire led to the creation of new countries in the Middle East, again without regard to the opinions of the people who lived there. Some of the long-term consequences of these decisions will be discussed below.

Russian Revolution of 1917: Russians had been discontented with their government for a long time. At the beginning of the twentieth century, Russia was one of the poorest, most backward countries in Europe. In 1905, Japan defeated Russia in the **Sino-Russian (Chinese-Russian) War.** The Japanese victory was the first Asian defeat of a European power in centuries, and Russia's humiliation contributed to a 1905 revolution that tried and failed to overthrow **Czar Nicholas II.** His reign lasted until 1917, when a second revolution, sparked partly by opposition to Russia's involvement in World War I, forced him to abdicate (leave) the throne. The czar and his family were executed by the revolutionaries. The new government, led by **Vladimir Lenin** and the communist **Bolshevik** party, signed a peace treaty with Germany in 1918 on terms that gave large amounts of Russian territory to Germany.

Russian Civil War (1917–1922): Lenin's Bolshevik government had a number of enemies in Russia. Groups that opposed the Russian Revolution formed a loose coalition called the "**White Guard**" and fought a civil war against the **Bolshevik Red Army.** The Whites lost because they were poorly organized and lacked a compelling vision for how Russia should be governed. In 1922, the victorious Bolsheviks announced the formation of the **Union of Soviet Socialist Republics (USSR),** made up of Russia, Ukraine, and other territories that had been part of the Russian

Empire. During the 1920s and 1930s, there was a lot of support for the Soviet Union in the United States and Europe; this changed once people began to learn about the large-scale imprisonment and murder of anyone who disagreed with the communist government.

United States (1919–1929)

First Red Scare* (1919–1920): The United States had been the site of communist and anarchist protests and plots since the 1880s, and the success of the Russian Revolution stirred up fears that a communist revolution could occur in the United States as well. After World War I ended, rising unemployment and continued immigration from Europe heightened tensions between capitalists and labor union leaders. Labor unions were seen as hotbeds of communist activity, and their leaders were generally suspected of wanting to take away the right of capitalists to own property. Newspapers published anti-communist propaganda that claimed that communism threatened to destroy the American way of life. Most European immigrants at this time were Catholics from Italy, Ireland, and Eastern Europe, and the white Protestants who ran America didn't see them as good candidates for American citizenship. Laws were passed to limit the immigration of Asians and Eastern Europeans.

* | The second Red Scare took place after World War II and is discussed below.

Race and Racism: The United States Armed Forces were segregated during World War I. African American soldiers fought overseas in their own units, and they acquitted themselves (performed) with honor and distinction. They also discovered in France a society without the racism and segregation they had experienced back home. When black veterans who had fought to defend democracy overseas returned home, they were often attacked and even killed by white mobs. The summer of 1919 is called the "**Red Summer**" because bloody race riots took place in several major American cities, including Chicago and Washington, DC. **SAT READING** has included passages about racism, lynching, and civil rights by writers such as **Alain Locke, W. E. B. Du Bois, James Weldon Johnson,** and **Ida B. Wells.**

Black Wall Street: More than fifty all-black towns were established between 1865 and 1920. When Oklahoma became a state in 1907, white settlers passed segregation laws almost immediately. In 1915, Oklahoma became the first state to require racially segregated pay telephones.

By the end of World War I, a prosperous all-black neighborhood known as **Greenwood** had developed in Tulsa, Oklahoma. Known as **Black Wall Street**, it boasted stores, churches, doctor's offices, hotels, and theaters. In 1921, a white mob attacked Greenwood on a two-day spree of looting, arson and violence. Hundreds of African Americans were murdered—mass graves have been found in recent years—and the entire neighborhood became a wasteland. The city of Tulsa suppressed news of the riots and hastened to assure white settlers that its "problems" had been resolved. For decades, Oklahoma history books omitted all mention of the riots, but in recent years, survivors and historians have worked to expose the truth. As a result, a passage about Black Wall Street or the Greenwood riots could appear on SAT WRITING.

African Americans were not the only "racial other" that white supremacists of the time hated and feared. Irish, Jewish, and Italian immigrants were equally unwelcome. Fears that these newcomers would overrun the country invigorated the Ku Klux Klan (KKK), a white supremacist group that had been founded at the end of the Civil War in 1865. During the 1920s, in addition to targeting African Americans, the KKK organized boycotts and raids of Catholic-owned businesses. They also targeted Irish, Italian, and Jewish people, none of whom were seen as "white" in America at this time (regardless of what they actually looked like).

Great Migration: Between 1916 and 1970, six million African Americans left extreme poverty, segregation and racial violence* in the South for better lives in Northern cities such as Baltimore, Detroit, Cleveland, New York, and Chicago. They reshaped major American cities, entered new professions and the arts, and became politically active. However, they also had to combat racism from white people who objected to living or working alongside them, and that sometimes led to violence. Racist housing policies segregated black people in ghettos, and both newly arrived European immigrants and all-white labor unions viewed them as undesirable competition for jobs.

* Almost 3,500 African Americans were lynched (hanged by racist mobs) between 1882 and 1968.

Flag flown from the New York City headquarters of the National Association for the Advancement of Colored People (NAACP), circa (about) 1923.

Harlem Renaissance: The **Harlem Renaissance** refers to the 1920s flowering of African American music, art and literature that was centered in the Harlem neighborhood of New York City. The educator **Alain Locke** is credited as its founder because he published an illustrated anthology (collection of short texts) of African American poetry, fiction, music, and theater that introduced many important black artists to a wider audience. **A. Philip Randolph** organized the first African American labor union, the **Brotherhood of Sleeping Car Porters**, and helped unionize large numbers of black workers. Writers such as **Langston Hughes, W. E. B. Du Bois, Zora Neale Hurston, Richard Wright,** and **Nella Larsen** wrote—and sometimes disagreed about—the meaning of race, solutions to racism, and the role of politics in art. Harlem Renaissance musicians whose work could be discussed in SAT WRITING passages include **Count Basie, Marian Anderson, Louis Armstrong, Billie Holiday,** and **Bessie Smith.** Visual artists whose work could be discussed include painters **Romare Bearden, Sargent Claude Johnson,** and **Miguel Covarrubias.**

A cartoon by Miguel Covarrubias.

Prohibition (1920–1933): The **Eighteenth Amendment** to the Constitution prohibited (outlawed) the production, importation, transportation, and sale of alcoholic beverages in the United States. However, it was not illegal to store alcohol, so many people stocked up while they still could. Once the law took effect, criminal gangs from cities such as New York, Philadelphia, and Chicago competed to supply the thirsty public. These enterprises bribed politicians and police officers, engaged in shoot-outs with each other and law enforcement, and even imported alcohol from Canada and the Caribbean. They also became fabulously rich.

The war against organized crime during the Prohibition Era was widely covered by the media of the time (newspapers and radio), and it has since generated many fiction and nonfiction books, movies and television shows. SAT READING literature passages have come from novels set during the Prohibition years, and SAT WRITING passages have discussed how the colorful personalities* of the era affected American popular culture.

   * | Including John Dillinger, Bugsy Siegel, Baby Face Nelson, Bonnie and Clyde, Pretty Boy Floyd, Machine Gun Kelly, and Ma Barker.

Women's Suffrage: British suffragists* (women who wanted the right to vote) who were jailed for their activism began to go on hunger strikes. The tactic gained publicity and support for the movement, especially after some women were held down and force-fed with tubes that were inserted up their noses and down into their stomachs by the prison authorities.

> * In the United States, **"suffragette"** was used as an insult. The suffix "-ette" feminized the word and was used to imply that suffragists were just a bunch of silly women.

The American feminists **Lucy Burns** and **Alice Paul** met in England, where they participated in women's suffrage demonstrations. They returned to the United States in 1917 and led about one thousand women in an eighteen-month-long protest in front of the White House.

Carrie Chapman Catt was less militant than Burns and Paul, and she focused her energy on supporting suffrage for women at the state level. She also traveled to advocate for women's rights internationally, and after World War I, to support pacifism (the belief that war is always unjustified). Excerpts from her many speeches have appeared on SAT READING.

The **Nineteenth Amendment** became law after it passed in both the House of Representatives and the Senate and was ratified (approved) by thirty-six states. It became the law of the land in time for the 1920 presidential election, in which eight million women voted for the first time.

> ✱ The thirty-sixth state to ratify the Nineteenth Amendment was Tennessee, and it was a closely contested vote. The deciding "yes" vote was cast by **Harry Burns**, a Tennessee legislator whose mother urged him in a letter to vote yes. This anecdote (story) has appeared in multiple test prep books and could easily be on SAT WRITING.

President **Warren G. Harding** also believed in full equality for African Americans and spoke out against the frequent lynchings that killed hundreds every year. His speeches on these topics could easily appear on SAT READING

Influenza Epidemic (1918–1920): Caused by an **H1N1 virus**, this strain of influenza infected about 500 million people, one-third of the world's population; 50 million people—about 10 percent of those infected—died. In the United States 675,000 people died. There was no flu vaccine, and antibiotics had not yet been developed. This pandemic is sometimes referred to as the **Spanish Flu**. Today, as the world grapples with the coronavirus pandemic, students should expect future SAT READING science passages about epidemiology.

Roaring Twenties: This decade saw many changes in how people lived. For the first time, more Americans lived in cities than on farms. New manufacturing and technology prospered, and America became wealthier than it had ever been before. People had money to spend, and there was a lot to spend it on, including labor-saving electric gadgets for newly electrified American homes.

Women benefited from the freedom that new technology brought. Electric appliances such as washing machines and vacuum cleaners shortened the hours that housework required, and store-bought clothing became more widely available and affordable. The new technologies of typing and stenography* created employment opportunities for women, so they were no longer relegated (confined) to housekeeping, sewing, nursing, and childcare jobs.

> * A system of shorthand (high-speed) writing used when taking dictation.

Radio provided a new way to pass leisure time and cinema made it possible for people in all parts of the country to share cultural experiences. It cost less than ten cents to see a movie, and about 75 percent of the population went to the movies at least once a week. The first "talkie" (movie with sound) was released in 1927. Passages about how this new technology changed the film industry have appeared on SAT WRITING.

The United States also became increasingly motorized. Cars became affordable, thanks to Henry Ford's moving assembly line, an innovation that reduced the assembly time for a Model T car from over twelve hours to ninety-three minutes. Production costs decreased as a result of saving so much time, and the price of a new Model T dropped to $260* by the middle of the decade. New industries in auto repair and auto parts sprang up, as did gas stations.

> * Worth about $3,400 in 2022.

Art Deco: An artistic movement that became popular in the 1920s for its use of bold geometrical shapes and sharp colors. It was used in architecture, advertising, calligraphy (decorative hand-writing), and interior design. The pictures below are intended to give you a sense of the look and feel of art deco in case you en-counter a passage about it on SAT WRITING.

Examples of art deco: (Clockwise) New York City's Chrysler Building; examples of art deco fonts; *Im Blau*, by Wassily Kandinsky; and *L'Aveu difficile*, by George Barbier.

Laissez-Faire Economics: The French phrase *laissez-faire* trans-lates as "let it be." Laissez-faire economists agreed with Adam Smith (above) that businesses should be allowed to operate without government regulations or oversight. This theory was often expressed in terms of natural selection (from Darwin's theory of evolution), so that the economy was portrayed as an ecosystem (network of interactive systems) in which brutal competition would ensure that only the "fittest" survived. Unfortunately, such a competitive environment did little to help small businesses defend themselves against large corporations. Monopolies dominated major industries, and the rights and protections of the middle and working classes were often ignored. High prices and low wages meant that the poor struggled to survive while the rich became richer.

Despite prosperity in manufacturing, American farmers struggled throughout the 1920s, and thousands lost their farms to bankruptcy. In addition, laissez-faire policies meant that the government did little to support trade unions that protected workers' wages and rights. This gave more power to the company owners and meant that workers suffered more.

Europe in the 1920s

Fascism: In 1919, **Benito Mussolini,** an Italian journalist-turned-politician conceived (created) fascism as an alternative to communism and democracy, which he believed had failed. He claimed that only a strong military dictatorship that strictly regimented (regulated) the economy and people's lives could lead Italy back to prosperity. Fascists promote nationalism (strong identification with one's country) and blame outsiders and minorities for their country's problems. Fascist governments stifle (silence) dissent, control and censor the media, and go to war to avenge the wrongs they believe their nation has suffered. They are also hostile to religion and notoriously indifferent (uncaring about) human rights.

Fascism had two important moments in the early 1920s. Benito Mussolini became Italy's dictator in 1922. In 1923, ultranationalist* leader **Adolf Hitler** staged the Beerhall Putsch, a failed fascist takeover of the German state of Bavaria. He was sentenced to five years in prison but only served nine months of his sentence. During that time, he wrote *Mein Kampf* (*My Struggle*), in which he blamed German Jews** for all of Germany's problems and complained that the Treaty of Versailles had humiliated and punished Germany unfairly after the war. He also promoted his version of a racially pure and powerful Germany that would rebuild its empire into a Thousand-Year Reich (German for rule).

> * Ultranationalists believe that their own country is better and more important than all others.

> ** Hitler did not invent his racial theories. Anti-Semitism (hatred and fear of Jews) drew on hundreds of years of European anti-Semitism.

Germany struggled to recover from the war. Germans felt humiliated after their country's defeat, and they resented the reparations and military limitations* that had been imposed by the Treaty of Versailles. German unemployment was high throughout the 1920s, war casualties had left many families without a male breadwinner (wage earner), and inflation (rising prices) made their money nearly worthless. These factors made the **Great Depression** of the 1930s especially severe in Germany and led to the rise of **Adolf Hitler** and his **Nazi Party**.

> * Germany ignored the limitations on its military and began to rebuild its forces in secret almost immediately.

National Socialist German Workers' (NAZI) Party: Although the full name of this nationalist political party contains the word "socialist," the Nazis were only socialist when it meant encouraging people to place the welfare of the state above their own needs. They focused on furthering the nationalist goals of the German state as it remilitarized and prepared to avenge (take revenge for) the suffering imposed on them by the Treaty of Versailles. The Nazis glorified absolute obedience to an authoritarian ruler, love of one's country and white racial superiority. They believed that Jews and other ethnic and religious minorities were inferior to those of "Aryan*" blood and studied the United States' segregation laws to get ideas about how to segregate Jews from the rest of German society.

*   "Aryan" originally referred to a prehistoric group of Indo-Europeans (white people who lived in northern and eastern India and eastern Europe). The idea of an "Aryan race" of light-skinned Indo-Europeans became popular in the mid-nineteenth century, when white scientists tried to prove that white people were biologically superior to those of other races. Nazi leader Adolf Hitler borrowed this idea when he used "Aryan" to mean white Europeans from Germany, Scandinavia, England, and the Netherlands.

The Great Depression (1929–1939)

The United States banking system was not well protected or regulated during the 1920s. Small and midsize banks were not insured by the federal government, so there was no backup if they didn't have enough money on hand to meet demand. When the banks had bad debts (for example, when a farmer couldn't make loan payments), they had no way to replace the money they lost.

Stock Market: Starting or expanding a business often requires a large up-front investment of capital (money). Owners can raise that money by selling "stock" (part-ownership shares) to investors, who are hoping that the value of the company—and therefore the value of each share of stock—will rise in the future. However, if a company's value shrinks, its investors end up with shares that are less valuable than they were at the time of purchase. When this happens, investors may rush to sell their now-less-valuable stock before its value decreases even more.

Stock values rose throughout the Roaring Twenties, and many people believed that they would never decline. At the same time, America's growing manufacturing sector offered easy credit with low interest rates for cars, homes and household appliances. As a result, people invested and bought on credit, often more than they could afford. Stock prices rose so fast that stock sold for far more than it was worth, creating a **bubble*** in the stock market. When the bubble "bursts," prices drop, and people panic and try to sell their stock before prices drop lower. This causes more people to try to sell, and prices drop even lower.

* The Dutch tulip craze of the early 1600s, one of the most famous examples of a financial bubble, has been discussed in SAT WRITING passages.

Stock Market Crash of 1929: During the summer of 1929, the **United States Federal Reserve** tried to slow the rapid rise of the stock market by increasing interest rates. This made credit more expensive, which in turn slowed the economy. People stopped buying homes and other expensive items. Businesses could not sell what they had purchased, so they couldn't pay their creditors (people they owed money to). Those creditors were then unable to pay their own expenses and debts, creating a ripple effect of lost income, businesses and jobs throughout the country. Passages discussing this widening spiral of economic loss have appeared on SAT READING.

Stock prices began to fall in September 1929, and panic set in among stockholders. Last-minute efforts by bankers and investment companies stabilized it for a few days, but on October 28, prices dropped even lower. On October 29, known as **Black Tuesday**, over sixteen million shares were traded—at very low prices—and billions of dollars were lost. Thousands of investors lost everything.

Many banks had to close because they ran out of money. People lost their life savings, and the ripples that had begun the previous summer affected growing numbers of people. Businesses' unpaid debts and inability to pay for ongoing expenses meant that other businesses lost money, so more people lost their jobs. Similarly, when people quit buying, manufacturers stopped producing, so everyone along the entire supply chain suffered financially. There have been multiple SAT READING passages about laissez-faire economics as well as sets of paired passages about whether governments are obligated (required) to prevent businesses from becoming too predatory (aggressive).

Today, people are routinely taught that ignoring drops in the stock market is often the safest course of action because the stocks will probably be worth more again in the future. However, not many knew this during the 1920s.

The Great Depression affected almost every country in the world because the international stock market meant that what happened in one country affected the others. France, Germany, the Netherlands, Australia, Canada, and the United Kingdom were still weak from World War I, and Germany was especially hard hit. Great Britain and France could not repay the United States for their wartime loans because Germany had fallen behind in its reparations payments to them. Unemployment in the United States hit 33 percent, and European nations had about 20 percent. Worldwide, manufacturing declined, prices dropped, banks failed, and millions of people lost their jobs and became homeless. Death rates soared because people could not get the food, warmth or medical care they needed to survive.

Dust Bowl: The economic hardship caused by the stock market crash was exacerbated (made worse) by several major droughts (prolonged periods of unusually low rainfall) in the United States during the 1930s. These droughts dried the soil that had been already depleted by poor farming methods in states such as Oklahoma, Nebraska, Arizona, Texas, and Kansas. Since these areas are mostly flat and prone to high winds, this dry soil was blown into the air, where it formed enormous dust storms that destroyed almost fifty million acres of crops across thirteen states and endangered the nation's ability to feed itself. Public protests and strikes broke out over high food prices as well as over the destruction of crops and livestock by farmers who couldn't sell their products at a profit.

President Franklin D. Roosevelt: The Depression began when **President Herbert Hoover** was in office. He was blamed for laissez-faire policies that made the Depression worse. Among other things, Hoover was blamed for mismanaging camps for the homeless; these camps were called **Hoovervilles** because they were seen as examples of government bungling (mismanagement) at a time of desperate need.

When Roosevelt took office in 1932, he responded decisively to the Great Depression. He proclaimed a "bank holiday" to stop people from withdrawing all of their money until the banks could restock their cash reserves. He also instituted the **New Deal**, a large stimulus program that was designed to restart the economy. It provided unemployment insurance to the unemployed, fed the hungry, and taught farmers better land management techniques.

President Roosevelt strongly supported civil rights for all Americans, and he appointed many influential leaders, including **Mary McLeod Bethune**, who promoted education for African American girls and was the first black female presidential adviser. Many of Roosevelt's white appointees were also progressive for their time. **Frances Perkins** became the first female Secretary of Labor.

Fireside Chats: President Roosevelt maximized the potential of radio technology by broadcasting a series of "**Fireside Chats**" that explained his policies for fighting the Depression, and later, the United States' progress in World War II (below). Several of these chats have been used for SAT READING passages. If you encounter one, remember that they were widely praised for boosting the morale of the country and for their clear, simple explanations of complex events and policies.

Works Progress Administration (WPA): The WPA put eight million of the country's over eleven million unemployed people back to work. Its construction projects built roads, bridges, and airports. **The Tennessee Valley Authority (TVA)** built hydroelectric dams to control flooding and produce cheap, reliable electricity. The national park system was expanded. Unemployed musicians and artists were paid to produce uniquely "American" art that would cultivate (encourage) national pride. Writers and historians were hired to travel throughout the South to interview formerly enslaved, mostly illiterate African Americans, so that there would be a record of their lives. SAT WRITING could include passages about some of these many projects.

Great Depression in Europe: After Germany lost World War I, the German emperor, **Kaiser Wilhelm II,** fled to the Netherlands to avoid being hanged by the French for his alleged (supposed) war crimes. His hasty departure from Germany caused political turmoil between factions advocating (speaking for) different ideas about how Germany should be governed. The German military favored a return to monarchy, but other groups supported democracy, socialism, communism, or fascism. Eventually, the democratic "**Weimar Republic**" (a new name for the German Empire) was established.

Twenty percent of the German population was unemployed in 1929, and that number tripled by 1933. People were poor, hungry, and desperate. High unemployment leads to social unrest because people who are out of work have no money and nothing to do all day. However, unlike today, when people hunt for jobs online from the comfort of home, back then they stood in line at unemployment offices or went door-to-door looking for work. Hungry people lined up at soup kitchens. All that standing around—reading newspaper headlines, listening to the radio, and talking to one another throughout the long, hungry, depressing days—created a perfect environment for people to share their dissatisfaction with the government for not helping people in such terrible times.

In the German election of 1932, the Nazi party became the largest in the Reichstag (German parliament), and Hitler, the party leader, was appointed German chancellor (like a prime minister) in January 1933. He quickly gained control of the entire German government through a combination of guile (sneakiness) and violence. Once in power, he began to oppress Germany's Jewish citizens as well as communists, all non-white races, people identifying as LGBTQ+, and the Roma*. He also instituted the murder of mentally and physically disabled people in hospitals and mental institutions throughout Germany, a project that involved many doctors and that ultimately killed about 275,000 people.

> * An itinerant (nomadic, wandering) group of Indo-Europeans. In English-speaking countries, they are also known as **gypsies**, a term that has often been used as a racial slur.

Hitler said that Germans needed *lebensraum* (living room), and that they needed to retake the eastern territory they had lost to Russia when they lost World War I. None of Germany's former opponents in the war wanted to hear that a new threat to European peace and stability was rising in Germany. England and France knew they were unprepared to fight another war because they were still weak from World War I, so they instead tried to prevent war at any cost. As a result, many leaders chose to believe Hitler's peaceful words instead of paying attention to his actions. In 1937, **Neville Chamberlain** became Britain's prime minister, and he strongly believed that the best policy for managing Adolf Hitler was "appeasement" (giving one's opponents what they want to keep them happy).

'Remember . . . One More Lollypop, and Then You All Go Home!'

Beloved children's author, Theodor Seuss Geisel (Dr. Seuss),
also worked as a political cartoonist in the 1930s. Here,
he responds to European appeasement of Germany.

One of the few politicians willing to speak out against Chamberlain's policy of appeasement was **Winston Churchill**. Churchill had risen to national prominence as a journalist in the Boer Wars (see above).

Out of political favor in the 1930s, Churchill spent several years as a lonely outsider. No one seemed to be listening as he inveighed (ranted) against Chamberlain's appeasement policy and predicted that it would end in catastrophe. Not surprisingly, when he turned out to be right, he was elected prime minister, a position he held throughout World War II. His speeches are eloquent defenses of democratic ideals, and at least one speech makes a persuasive case for American support of the British. Churchill's speeches are frequently excerpted on SAT READING.

World War II (1939–1945)

There is a lot of information about World War II because more has been written about it than any other war. The information provided here is at best a highlight reel, but I have also included some of the often-overlooked stories of the war, such as the United States' internment (imprisonment) of Japanese Americans, because the campaigns to right these wrongs have often been passage topics for SAT WRITING.

World War II took place on every continent except Antarctica. More than fifty countries and seventy million people participated in the fighting. Between seventy-five and eighty-five million soldiers and civilians were killed. Great empires were destroyed. Millions of people from various minority groups were targeted for enslavement, including six million Jews who were suffocated in gas chambers or otherwise killed. Wartime science led to better ways to kill people, including the atom bomb, the deadliest weapon invented up until that time.

Invasion of Poland (1939): In a move called the *Anschluss*, Germany annexed Austria, creating a "Greater Germany" in accordance with popular desire in both countries. Although the move was in clear violation of the Treaty of Versailles, no European nation objected. This emboldened Hitler to annex the Sudetenland region of Czechoslovakia, claiming that its many German speakers proved that it, too, belonged within the historic boundaries of Greater Germany. He then used his foothold in the Sudetenland to invade the rest of Czechoslovakia. Again, no European power objected. In August 1939, Germany and Russia signed a nonaggression pact, promising not to attack each other.

On September 1, 1939, Germany invaded Poland from the west. Russia invaded from the east on September 17. The Polish army was defeated within weeks, and Germany and Russia divided Poland between them. England and France declared war on Germany two days after it invaded Poland, but they did so little that the press made fun of them for declaring a "Phoney (fake) War."

Poland was divided by two conquerors after September 1939.

Blitzkrieg: The German technique of **blitzkrieg** (lightning war) involved quick strikes by rapidly moving aircraft, tanks, and artillery units. It allowed the Germans to conquer Norway, Denmark*, Belgium, the Netherlands, Luxembourg, France, Yugoslavia, and Greece in under two years.

* The Danish people saved 90 percent of the country's Jews from the Holocaust and smuggled many of them to neutral Sweden. You may have read Lois Lowry's historical novel, *Number the Stars*, in which a Christian family participates in the Danish resistance and helps its Jewish friends escape the Nazis.

When the *blitzkrieg* or *blitz* invaded Denmark in April 1940, the Danish king quickly negotiated a surrender. The Germans then used Denmark as a staging ground for their invasion of Norway ten days later. After defeating the Norwegian army, the Germans established a puppet government* headed by Norwegian fascist **Vidkun Quisling**, whose last name quickly became synonymous with "collaborator" (someone who helps an enemy conqueror).

> ✳ A government in which the officials of a country appear to be ruling as usual while really obeying their conquerors.

Miracle at Dunkirk: By May, the German *blitz* reached the "Low Countries" (the Netherlands*, Luxembourg, and Belgium) and France. British, French, Belgian, and Canadian troops were forced to retreat to the beaches of **Dunkirk**, a coastal city in the north of France, where they were quickly surrounded by German forces. The British Royal Navy launched a rescue operation by sea that involved hundreds of naval and civilian vessels, including small fishing boats, that succeeded in evacuating 38,000 British and Allied soldiers across the English Channel to safety in England. This daring rescue bolstered (raised) British spirits at a time when a German invasion of the British Isles seemed imminent (about to happen). The 2017 movie *Dunkirk* portrays these events.

> ✳ Anne Frank, who wrote *Diary of a Young Girl*, lived in Amsterdam, the capital of the Netherlands.

1942 was the "high tide" of German power.

Winston Churchill was elected prime minister of Britain in May 1940 and oversaw the evacuation of Dunkirk. His May 13 speech to Parliament has been used as an SAT READING passage. In it, Churchill warns that a long, hard struggle is ahead and says that he has nothing to offer the British people except "blood, toil, tears and sweat." He says that Britain is fighting "a monstrous tyranny, never surpassed in the dark, lamentable catalog of human crime" and that their only goal is "victory at all costs because without victory, there is no survival."

Following the successful evacuation from Dunkirk, Churchill gave another speech that has also been used for SAT READING. In it, he reminds listeners that there have already been over thirty thousand British casualties and that the defeat of France and Belgium is a "colossal military disaster" that puts Britain in great danger of invasion. He says that there has never been a successful invasion* of the British Isles, and that he has confidence in the British people's resolve.

*   This is not strictly true. Churchill omits the Roman invasion of 42 AD and the Norman Conquest of 1066.

The speech ends with Churchill's rousing declaration that no matter what happens, ". . . we shall not flag or fail. We shall go on to the end, we shall fight in France, we shall fight on the seas and oceans . . . whatever the cost may be, we shall fight on the beaches, we shall fight on the landing grounds, we shall fight in the fields and in the streets, we shall fight in the hills; we shall never surrender."

Battle of Britain: In June 1940, the French government surrendered to the Germans, and Italy entered the war on Germany's side. In July, the Germans launched the Battle of Britain, three months of almost nightly bombing attacks, hoping to prepare the way for a ground invasion. However, the British Royal Air Force was able to inflict enough damage on Germany's *Luftwaffe* (air force) that Hitler changed his mind about trying to invade.

Vichy France: After France surrendered, the Germans installed a puppet government known as Vichy France after the town in which it had its headquarters. It collaborated with the Nazis and supported their efforts to round up French Jews for deportation or death.

Operation Barbarossa: In June 1941, Germany violated its non-aggression pact with the Soviet Union and invaded with a force of over three million troops spread out over two thousand miles. By December, it had become the battle with the largest number of casualties in human history: over seven million casualties, most of whom were Russian. However, the Soviet Union was eventually able to force the invaders back, leaving the Germans fighting on two fronts.

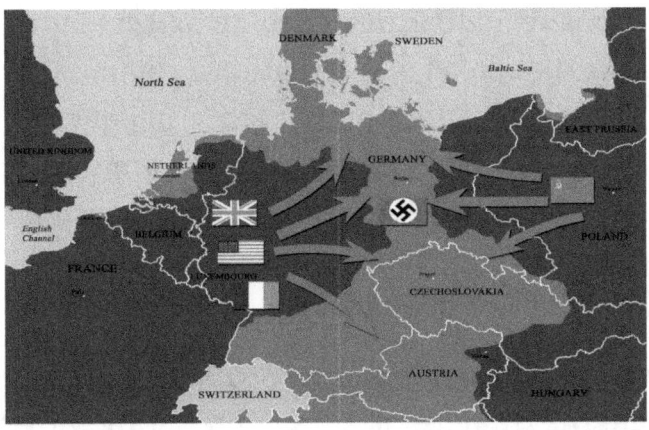

Germany's position after the failure of Operation Barbarossa.

Japan (1929-1939): Japan is an island nation with a long history of hostility to foreigners. It joined the Allied Powers during World War I, but it sided with the Axis Powers in World War II because it wanted to control Asia the way Germany controlled Europe. Many in the Japanese government and military believed that Japanese people were racially superior to people in the rest of Asia.

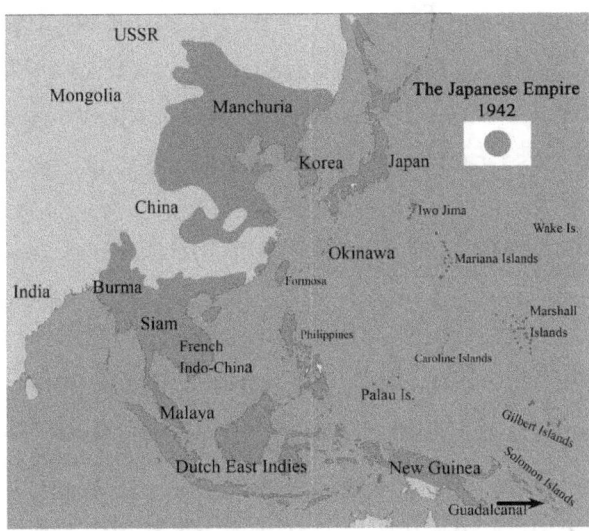

The Empire of Japan in 1942.

In 1936, Germany and Japan signed an agreement to stand together against the spread of international communism. In 1937, Japan invaded China and captured three important cities: Beijing, Shanghai, and Nanjing. The Japanese army gained a reputation for brutality in the "Rape of Nanjing," which involved the systematic rape of tens of thousands of Chinese women and the slaughter of about 300,000 captured civilians.

Attack on Pearl Harbor (December 7, 1941): The Japanese wanted to prevent the United States from interfering with their plans to conquer Asia and the Pacific Islands. Early in the morning of December 7, Japan bombed Pearl Harbor, the United States naval base in Hawaii, killing about 2,500 and destroying a significant portion of the American naval fleet. By the time President Roosevelt asked Congress to declare war the next day, Japan had also attacked two United States naval bases in the Philippines, capturing its capital city of Manila as well as the British colony of Malaya and the United States territory of Guam. Roosevelt's speech to Congress is famous for its opening words, "Yesterday, December 7, 1941, a date which will live in infamy*, the United States of America was suddenly and deliberately attacked by naval and air forces of the Empire of Japan."

* Infamy: Fame for doing something bad.

Many news reports that commemorate the anniversary of the attack on Pearl Harbor each year quote Roosevelt's description of the attack, and it could easily turn up as an SAT READING passage. At the end of the speech, Congress voted to declare war on Japan. In response, Germany honored its alliance with Japan and declared war on the United States, which declared war on Germany on December 11, 1941.

United States Mobilizes for War: The attack on Pearl Harbor was a major military defeat for the United States. The declarations of war on Japan and Germany meant it now needed to rebuild the badly damaged Pacific fleet and recruit, equip and train a much larger fighting force. Between December 1941 and the war's end in August 1945, the United States Armed Forces grew from 2.2 million people to over 16 million. However, by the time the Battle of Britain started, President Roosevelt realized that the United States would have to aid the beleaguered (desperate) Allies with money and war supplies. He implemented the **"lend-lease program"** to loan money and equipment to the Allies. Roosevelt also deployed the American Navy to protect English ships from German attacks; shots were fired in the Atlantic Ocean months before the 1941 Japanese attack on Pearl Harbor, and German submarines attacked and sank American merchant ships within a few miles of America's east coast.

The short version of the Pacific war is that Japan won every battle between December 1941 and June 1942. The Japanese military's reputation for cruelty was reinforced by its brutal treatment or prisoners of war and for forcing thousands of women from the countries it conquered to work as "comfort women" (sex slaves) for the Japanese military.

Battle of Attu: The **Aleutian Islands** are part of Alaska. In June 1942, the Japanese captured two of them, **Kiska** and **Attu**, and occupied them until May 1943, when they were retaken in an extremely bloody battle that left about 550 American soldiers and over 2,500 Japanese troops dead. Kiska and Attu are the only parts of America that fell under enemy control during World War II, and the battle to reclaim them for the United States would make an excellent topic for an SAT WRITING passage.

Bataan Death March: In April 1942, the Japanese military won the **Battle of Bataan** (in the Phillipines) and forced about 75,000 American and Filipino prisoners of war on an arduous (difficult) march through the jungle. Thousands died from the effects of starvation, disease, and injuries, while others were killed for being too weak to walk on their own.

Battle of Midway (June, 1942): The Battle of Midway was an important turning point in the war against Japan. Midway is an atoll (small island made of coral) in the middle of the Pacific Ocean. The United States won a two-day battle against Japanese forces that left Japan on a defensive footing for the rest of the war.

Home Front: The war economy meant that production of other goods slowed or stopped entirely. Food producers now prioritized (put first) feeding the armed forces, so the government encouraged people to plant "Victory gardens" and preserve what they grew to meet their families' needs. Tires and automotive parts were unavailable to civilians, as were toasters, washing machines, and other domestic appliances. Auto factories stopped making cars and instead produced tanks, planes, and military vehicles such as trucks and jeeps. Gasoline was rationed, as were sugar, coffee, butter, and meat. Scrap metal was salvaged for use in military gear.

Messages like these encouraged Americans
at home to support rationing.

As the posters above suggest, the media played an important role in the war effort. Working with the government, Hollywood produced films with patriotic messages and uplifting themes, and the newsreels shown before feature films in movie theaters often included front line footage and heartwarming stories about those fighting overseas. The comic book characters **Wonder Woman** and **Captain America** were created in 1941 to fight on the side of democracy. SAT WRITING passages could discuss these cultural developments and their impact on the war effort.

Internment of Japanese Americans: Although the majority of Americans at that time agreed that Japanese Americans were an active danger to the United States after the bombing of Pearl Harbor, the United States' treatment of Japanese Americans is now considered a significant human rights violation. Anti-Japanese prejudice was already high in the United States, and the Japanese attacks raised suspicions that Japanese Americans would collude (conspire) with Japan to undermine the American war effort. Within hours of the bombing of Pearl Harbor, the United States Justice Department had arrested hundreds of Japanese business and community leaders and frozen all of their financial assets. President Roosevelt ordered the internment of the entire Japanese American community into ten different concentration camps. Canada and Mexico also arrested people of Japanese descent and sent them to camps in the United States.

THIS IS THE ENEMY

Racist imagery was common in anti-Japanese propaganda after the attack on Pearl Harbor.

Despite the hardships that the detainees suffered in the camps, 33,000 American men of Japanese descent fought in the United States Armed Forces during the war. The 13,000-member all-Japanese 100th/442nd Infantry Regiment became the most-decorated unit of its size in American military history. When the war ended and the detainees were finally allowed to leave the camps, many found that white people had claimed their homes and businesses. Anti-Japanese groups claimed that the Japanese were racially inferior and naturally untrustworthy and even tried to revoke the citizenship of American-born Japanese.

Images like this one were common in 1945.

In 1988, President Ronald Reagan apologized to the Japanese American community for America's treatment during the war and acknowledged that it had been "solely based on race." At that time, living survivors of the camps were each awarded $20,000 in reparations (compensation) for the years, homes, businesses, and savings they had lost.

Women During World War II: The Japanese attack on Pearl Harbor inflicted massive damage on the United States Navy. Suddenly, the United States was at war. The defense industry needed to expand to meet the needs of this new military, but there were not enough men left in the workforce to meet the demand. About one-fourth of women already worked outside the home, and even more were needed.

Seventy-five years after WWII ended, Rosie the Riveter
remains a popular image of female strength.

The "**Rosie the Riveter**" advertising campaign was intended to persuade middle-class white women to work in the badly understaffed defense industry. The need was so great that Congress allocated (set aside) twenty million dollars to build childcare facilities where working mothers could leave their children. Cities swelled and "boom towns" sprang up as workers relocated their families to be near their jobs. Boarding houses rented rooms and served hot meals to women who worked all day. Although African American women were included in the wartime workforce, they were often the last hired and lowest paid of all workers, even when they did the same work.

Segregation in the United States Armed Forces: The United States military was racially segregated during World War II. Japanese Americans fought in their own units (above), but black soldiers were not even trained to fight. Instead, they worked as cooks, maintenance workers, and support staff. As white combat troop casualties rose, however, black soldiers were pressed into combat, and both individual black soldiers and all-black units earned many medals for their heroism and bravery during the war.

President Roosevelt signed a law that forbade racial or religious discrimination in the defense industry in 1941. Black colleges and universities received federal funding, increased enrollment and added courses that trained a generation of African American engineers, mathematicians, mechanics, and technicians. Many companies in the American South and Southwest refused to hire black people, so many graduates of wartime training programs were forced to relocate to the West Coast or Northeastern United States to find work.

Tuskegee Airmen: In addition to believing that black people made poor soldiers, many white Americans believed they were not smart enough to be pilots. Fearing a shortage of trained pilots if war broke out, President Roosevelt gave in to pressure from the **National Association for the Advancement of Colored People (NAACP)**, the African American press, and his wife, Eleanor, to open the civilian training program to include African Americans. The president knew that about one-third of the white American voting public believed in white supremacy, and he was reluctant to anger these constituents by helping African Americans. Finally, the program was approved, and a training program was set up at the Tuskegee Airfield in Alabama.

However, the struggle of black aviators continued. Racism was as prevalent in the United States Army Air Corps* as it was in the rest of the United States, and some white officers actively opposed any kind of racial integration. However, the Tuskegee Airmen persisted in their belief that they had the right to fight for their country, and in the end, like their Japanese American counterparts, acquitted themselves with distinction. Their success contributed to the eventual desegregation of the American military in 1948. The movie *Red Tails* tells the story of the Tuskegee Airmen. Their story could be the focus of an SAT WRITING passage.

* | The Army Air Corps became the Air Force in 1947.

Double V for Victory: A few weeks after the bombing of Pearl Harbor, the editor of the *Pittsburgh Courier** wrote about the similarities between segregation in the United States and the treatment of Jews in Nazi Germany. The paper also printed—and then acted on—a letter from a reader that suggested turning the popular "V for Victory" sign into a double V so that one V stood for victory in the war and the other for victory over racism. The *Courier* then designed a logo that it published on its front page, and the double V was adopted as a sign of black patriotism and solidarity throughout the military and the country at large. Historians have traced many of the public expressions of black solidarity in athletics and elsewhere to the "Double V" campaign, so it could turn up as an SAT WRITING passage. SAT READING could include passages by African Americans advocating for the chance to demonstrate their patriotism more fully.

* | The largest black-owned newspaper in the United States.

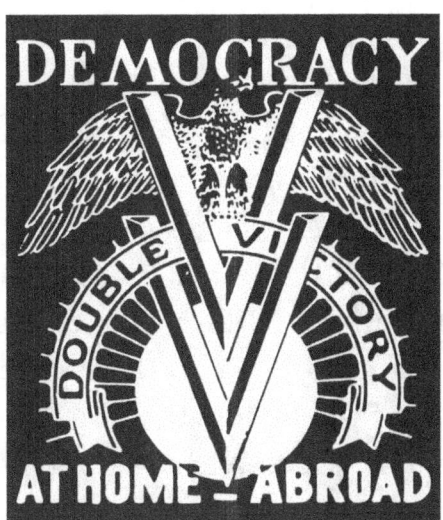

The "Double V" symbolized African Americans' dual commitment to winning the war overseas and defeating racism at home.

Navajo Code Talkers: "Navajo" is the name of a large Native American tribe and the name of its language, which has no written form. Only Navajo people speak it. Shortly after the United States declared war on Japan and Germany, the United States Marine Corps recruited the **Navajo Code Talkers**, a unit of Navajo/English speakers who could translate messages from one language to the other almost instantaneously. This had two advantages. First, messages that once took half an hour to encode and send now took less than a minute. Second, no one could crack the code because it was based on a language that the Axis powers may not even have known existed. At times, the Code Talkers actually spoke over unsecured phone lines. The Japanese could tap the phones and listen, but they could not understand anything. The Navajo code has still never been cracked, and the success of the Code Talkers, another patriotic minority who contributed to the war effort, would be a good topic for an SAT WRITING passage.

North African Campaign (1940–1943): Although the first American combat troops arrived in England in 1942, the Allies realized that they were not ready to mount a successful campaign to retake Europe. Instead, they turned their attention to North Africa, where Allied and Axis forces were engaged in a series of costly back-and-forth battles. When thousands of American and British troops landed in the North African country of Tunisia, their victory dealt a major blow to Germany and Italy and secured the oil fields of the Middle East for Allied use. The Allies went on to attack Italy, which Winston Churchill called the "soft underbelly of Europe."

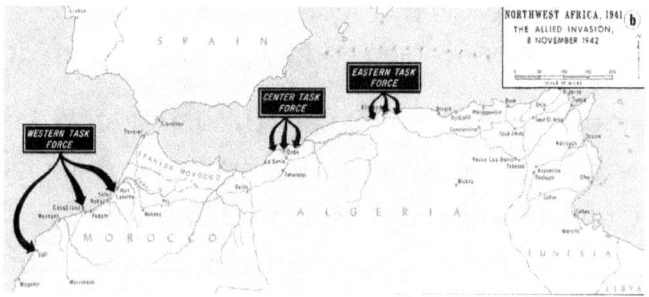

The arrows show Allied attacks on German-held North Africa.

Italy Drops Out (1943): After defeating the Axis in North Africa, the Allies retook the Italian island of Sicily, causing the collapse of Mussolini's government in Italy. By September, the Allies had landed in continental Italy. In October, the new Italian government declared war on Germany. However, there were German forces scattered throughout Italy, and they easily took control of the Italian government and disarmed the Italian army. The Allies then slogged it out with the Germans before finally achieving victory in May 1945.

D-Day (June 6, 1944): Code-named "Operation Overlord," the D-Day invasion of Normandy remains the largest naval invasion in history. Preparations for the invasion were extensive and elaborate. The Allies invented a fictitious (fake) army and faked evidence that convinced the Germans that they were planning to try to land at the French port in Calais, when they were really preparing to invade the beaches of Normandy three hundred miles to the south. The real invasion included extensive Allied bombing of German defenses along the beaches by over eleven hundred aircraft. This was followed by the landing of about five hundred Allied ships loaded with troops and equipment. Allied planes also transported 24,000 American, Canadian, and British troops, who used parachutes to land behind enemy lines the night before the attack began. Their mission was to prevent supplies and reinforcements from getting to Nazi troops.

When a force of over 150,000 American, Canadian, and British troops began leaving their vessels and waded ashore in Normandy, they did so under heavy fire that caused thousands of casualties. Many died in the water between their ships and the shore, and many more died on beaches from landmines the Germans had buried. Over 4,000 Allied soldiers lost their lives on the first day of the invasion.

Despite high casualties, by the end of June 1944, the Allies had successfully landed about 2.5 million men, 4 million tons of supplies, and 500,000 trucks and tanks. By the end of August, they had retaken northern France and liberated Paris. From then until the German surrender in May 1945, the Germans fought a defensive war, trying to slow the Allies as they advanced toward Berlin.

Battle of the Bulge: On December 16, 1944, the Germans mounted a surprise attack that was intended to break through the Allied lines and drive them out of Europe. It was a well-planned offensive that included using English-speaking German soldiers in stolen Allied equipment and uniforms to penetrate Allied lines. American soldiers responded by interrogating suspected infiltrators about baseball and American pop culture.

The United States **101st Airborne Division** was besieged for two weeks before help arrived. Soldiers trapped in the forest suffered extreme cold, frostbite, pneumonia and other "cold injuries." However, the Germans ultimately failed to break through the Allied lines, and their loss led them to surrender in May 1945*.

> * These events are depicted in Stephen E. Ambrose's book, *Band of Brothers*, which was made into an HBO miniseries.

President Roosevelt died of a cerebral hemorrhage a few months into his fourth term as president, just a few months before Germany surrendered. Vice president **Harry S Truman*** became president and oversaw the end of the war. In 1947, Congress passed the **Twenty-Second Amendment**, which says that no one is allowed to serve more than two terms (eight years) as president. It was ratified and became law in 1951.

> * President Truman famously told reporters not to put a period after his middle initial because the S did not stand for any actual name.

When Germany surrendered in May 1945, Europe was in tatters. Over fifty million people had died and about sixty million refugees roamed Europe. The Jewish population, with six million dead, was one-third the size it had been in 1933. The Roma (gypsy) population was only a quarter of its former size. Entire cities had been destroyed and the economy was in ruins.

Atomic Bomb: Unlike Germany, Japan fought on despite repeated Allied demands that it surrender. The Allies embarked on an extensive campaign that included the firebombing of sixty-seven Japanese cities and bitter fighting to retake land the Japanese had captured. The Japanese resisted fiercely, even as civilians began to starve. Allied commanders began to fear that the campaign to end the Pacific War would be long and bloody.

In 1939, President Franklin D. Roosevelt was informed that German scientists were working on building an atomic bomb, and he authorized a group of United States scientists to conduct atomic research. In 1942, Roosevelt created the **Manhattan Project**, a secret group of scientists whose job was to build a bomb before the Germans did. They succeeded and exploded the first atomic bomb in an unpopulated desert area of New Mexico in 1945.

Convinced that American casualties would be high if the war against Japan continued, Truman authorized the atomic bombing of two Japanese cities, **Hiroshima** and **Nagasaki**, three days apart. Six days after the second bombing, on August 15, 1945, Japan surrendered, and World War II ended. By the time Japan surrendered, over three million people had died. Japan's economy and infrastructure (bridges, tunnels, and roads) were badly damaged and Japanese civilians suffered extreme hardship. The controversy continues to this day over whether Truman's decision was an atrocity or a justified act of war.

Holocaust and Other Atrocities: Genocide is the deliberate killing of an entire group of people. A "**holocaust**" is a great sacrifice or terrible tragedy. When capitalized, the word refers to Hitler's attempted genocide of European Jews. The Holocaust is also known by its Hebrew name, the Shoah, which is also the name of an award-winning documentary.

The Holocaust began in earnest in 1942, when the **Auschwitz death camp** in southern Poland began gassing thousands of Jews on a daily basis and burning the bodies in crematoria (places for burning the dead).

There were about 15 million Jews worldwide when Hitler came to power, and 9.5 million of them lived in Europe. Six million died—two out of every three European Jews—between 1933 and 1945, and these deaths are collectively known as the Holocaust. Also, in what's been called "the forgotten Holocaust," the Nazis killed between 500,000 and 1.5 million Roma out of a population of approximately 2 million. Throughout the war, they also persecuted and murdered communists, Jehovah's Witnesses, the disabled, and people who were LGBTQ+.

Slaughter on such a large scale had to be organized and systematic because all the bodies had to be disposed of. The Nazis experimented with various methods of mass slaughter before deciding that using gas chambers to kill and crematoria to dispose of the bodies was the most efficient. About 44,000 locations were used to intern people, including a number of labor camps and death camps that were established throughout Europe. These camps are generally called "concentration camps."

German death and labor camps dotted Germany and
German-held territory during World War II.

Not all World War II atrocities were committed by the Axis Powers. The Allied Powers—Great Britain, the United States, France,
the Soviet Union, and China—also committed atrocities that, although smaller in scale, are also an important part of the story.
The Allies firebombed* many German and Japanese cities, and
the United States interned Japanese Americans in concentration camps. The Soviet Union's military was poorly trained and
equipped, so it compensated for its lack of firepower by sending
millions of infantry (foot soldiers) into battle against the German army's tanks, planes, and superior artillery. As a result of
its lack of preparedness, the Soviet Union lost more than nine
million soldiers, a loss much greater than that suffered by any
other country.

* | The Allied firebombing of Dresden, Germany, is the
   | subject of Kurt Vonnegut's novel, *Slaughterhouse-
   | Five*.

PART II:
THE POSTWAR ERA (1945–1990)

Postcolonialism*

When World War II began in 1939, France, Britain, and Germany all had extensive empires in Asia, Africa, and the Middle East. Their colonies were pulled into the war because they provided resources and soldiers and because they were sometimes invaded by their colonizer's adversaries (enemies). Most colonies resented their second-class status and had well-established independence movements before the war began. Although many paused for the duration of the war, they reemerged when it ended. They were often inspired by the democratic ideals of the American Revolution and looked to the United States for assistance in achieving democratic self-government.

* | After colonial rule has ended.

It's important to understand postcolonialism for SAT READING. Literature passages often come from the work of important postcolonial writers, such as **Isabel Allende, Gabriel García Márquez, Chinua Achebe, Jamaica Kincaid,** and **Jhumpa Lahiri.** Historical passages may be taken from the speeches or writing of postcolonial leaders such as **Edward Said, Frantz Fanon, Mohandas Gandhi**, and **Nelson Mandela**. Understanding the general patterns of invasion, colonization, resistance, and independence can help you make smart inferences about texts set during conflicts you might not have studied.

United Nations (UN): The United Nations was founded in 1945, when representatives of fifty countries gathered in San Francisco to draft a charter (statement) for an international organization to work for world peace and universal human rights. It coordinates global responses to problems such as disease, war and natural disasters. It also provides humanitarian assistance, food, and medical care to hundreds of millions of people in over one hundred countries. Its peacekeeping forces provide security and stability in high-conflict regions all over the world. Many important speeches have been made at the UN in the almost eighty years of its existence, and those speeches frequently appear as SAT READING passages. In general, they emphasize the UN's commitment to universal human rights, world peace, and prosperity.

Indian Independence: The **Indian Independence Movement** began when India became a British colony in 1858 and included many riots and rebellions that the British put down with military force. During World War II, the British government insisted that India join the war as an ally, but many Indians resented being drawn into a war that they thought had nothing to do with them. Some Indians sided with the Axis Powers because they were fighting the British.

Mohandas Gandhi: Gandhi earned the title of **Mahatma*** for his leadership of the Indian independence movement. His political activism began in 1914, when he promoted nonviolent resistance to British rule, including hunger strikes, protest marches, refusal to pay taxes, letter-writing campaigns to British officials, and boycotts of British goods. After World War II ended, Gandhi's tactics added to the pressures caused by the war's economic impact and resulted in India's independence in 1947. His strategies also inspired other leaders, most notably **Martin Luther King, Jr.**, to resist injustice nonviolently. Speeches by Gandhi have appeared on **SAT READING**.

* | Mahatma is a title that means "wise leader."

Partition of India and Pakistan: The 1947 partition (separation) of India into **Hindu*** India and Muslim Pakistan was intended to avert (stop) religious conflict from breaking out once India became independent. However, implementing the mass migration of millions of people created one of the worst tragedies of the postwar era.

** | Hinduisim is the world's oldest religion and the third largest today. Its followers believe that there are multiple manifestations or avatars of God. They also believe in reincarnation.

In 1947, India was predominantly Hindu, but it was also home to sizable minorities of Muslims. There had been periodic wars between Muslims and Hindus in India since the late seventeenth century.

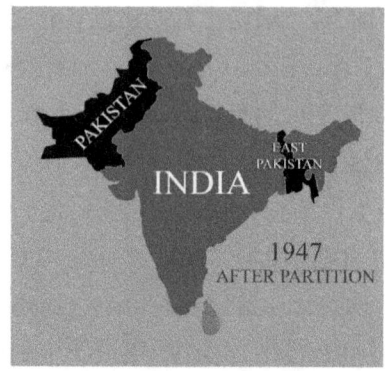

The results of partition. **East Pakistan** became the independent country of **Bangladesh** in 1971.

As soon as the British withdrew from India, a religious civil war broke out. Neighbors and family members attacked and killed one another. Over fourteen million Indians were forced to move from one country to the other. Muslims migrated from India to West Pakistan and East Pakistan—today's Pakistan and Bangladesh—while Hindus traveled in the reverse direction. Between two hundred thousand and two million people died. "Blood trains" of refugees were attacked en route and arrived at their destinations filled with corpses. As many as one hundred thousand Hindu and Muslim women were abducted and raped by men of the other religion.

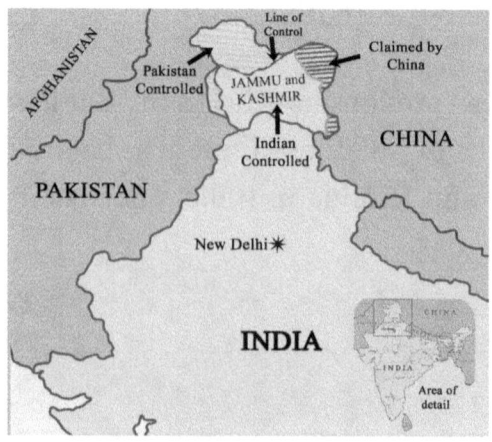

Partition also led to a dispute over Kashmir.

There have been four wars between India and Pakistan since Partition as well as numerous smaller conflicts, mostly over control of **Jammu** and **Kashmir**, predominantly Muslim regions that provide water and hydro-powered (water-powered) electricity to a billion people. As the map above shows, Pakistan was initially divided into an Indian zone and a Pakistani zone, although China claimed a small section of the region as well. Both India and Pakistan developed their own nuclear bombs in the early 1970s, and they engaged in a nuclear arms race in the 1990s. Today, tension between the two countries remains high, and violence flares up periodically.

Israeli Statehood: Israel was created partly in response to the decline of the British Empire's position in the Middle East. The term "**Middle East**" is generally understood to refer to fifteen countries* in western Asia, Egypt in northern Africa, and Turkey, which is mostly in Asia but has a small area in Europe as well. The Middle East is also known as Asia Minor, Mesopotamia, the Fertile Crescent, and the Cradle of Civilization.

> * Bahrain, Cyprus, Iran, Iraq, Israel, Jordan, Kuwait, Lebanon, Oman, Palestine, Qatar, Saudi Arabia, Syria, United Arab Emirates, and Yemen.

The Middle East was conquered by the Ottoman Empire at its height during the sixteenth century, but the empire's long decline began almost immediately afterward. The British and the French colonized much of its territory in the nineteenth century. Arab nationalist movements pressured the Ottoman Empire to reform and allow local populations to govern themselves, and the combination of external attacks and internal dissent shrank and weakened it even further. A revolution in 1908 was followed by war in 1912–1913. When World War I began in 1914, the much-weakened Ottoman Empire joined the Central Powers (Germany, Austria-Hungary, and Bulgaria).

Palestine: A strip of land between Syria and Egypt, the region of Palestine is significant to three major world religions—Judaism, Christianity, and Islam—and the site of four thousand years of religious and political warfare. It is also known as the **Holy Land, Canaan,** and the **Levant.** In general, texts that refer to Canaan or the Holy Land have a religious context, and those that refer to the Levant are speaking historically from a secular (nonreligious) perspective.

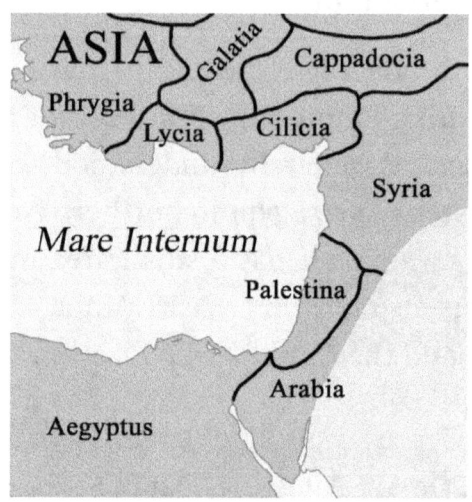

Palestine's location made it strategically important for conquest and trade.

Palestine's history includes 3,500 years of conquest and foreign rule that ended with the defeat of the Ottoman Empire. The Ottomans divided Palestine into different regions, but none of them was called Palestine. When nationalist groups developed in nineteenth-century Europe, their message of self-rule became popular in Palestine, as well as in the Middle East generally. However, Palestine was a region, not a country, and **Palestinian** did not yet refer to a national identity.

Zionism: Centuries of anti-Semitism had convinced many European Jews that assimilation (not looking or acting Jewish) was the best defense against religious persecution. **Theodor Herzl,** an Austrian Jew, disagreed. In 1896, Herzl published a pamphlet in which he argued that Jews were one people—a nation—that should be permitted to return to its "unforgettable historic homeland" in Palestine. Herzl believed that European Jews should move to **Zion,** one of the Biblical names for the ancient kingdom of Israel, and this gave his movement its name: **Zionism.**

Suez Canal: The 120-mile **Suez Canal** cuts through Egypt and connects the Mediterranean Sea and the Red Sea. In the 1870s, Egypt's financial difficulties led it to sell its share of the canal to the British. When World War I began in 1914, the Germans and Ottomans attacked the canal. They were driven back by the British, who then pushed forward into Palestine, Egypt's neighbor.

McMahon-Hussein Agreement: In 1915, British High Commissioner of Egypt **Henry McMahon** and **Hussein bin Ali,** sharif (religious leader) of **Mecca,*** exchanged a series of letters in which the United Kingdom promised to support Arab autonomy from the Ottoman Empire after the war. Palestinian Arabs interpreted the agreement as a British commitment to Palestinian independence.

> * The Ottoman Empire controlled **Mecca** and **Medina,** the two Islamic holy cities.

Sykes-Picot Agreement (1916): The French and British secretly agreed to divide Ottoman territories between themselves and their allies after they won the war. Many Arabs opposed the Sykes-Picot Agreement because it contradicted the

McMahon-Hussein Agreement's promise of support for Palestinian independence.

Balfour Declaration (1917): Arthur Balfour, the British foreign secretary (in charge of international relations), wrote a letter that expressed the British government's support of "the establishment in Palestine of a national home for the Jewish people" to **Lionel Rothschild**, a British baron (low-level noble) and president of a prominent organization of British Jews. However, Palestinian Arabs worried that a Jewish homeland would threaten their goal of self-rule. Despite their opposition, the **Balfour Declaration** was included in the 1919 Treaty of Versailles even though it clearly contradicted the 1915 McMahon-Hussein Agreement's commitment to support Arab nationalist movements after the defeat of the Ottoman Empire.

The Treaty of Versailles also honored the Sykes-Picot Agreement by establishing the **mandate system*** that gave the French and British authority over the Ottoman Empire's former territories. The **French Mandate** controlled the area that is now Syria, Lebanon, and northern Iraq, and the **British Mandate** covered southern Iraq, Palestine, and Jordan. Egypt became independent, with the exception of the British-owned Suez Canal. Iraq, Syria, and Lebanon all became independent before World War II began, but Palestine remained a British colony.

  * | Mandated territories are controlled, but not owned, by a foreign power. Colonized territories are owned.

When the British took control of Palestine under the British Mandate in 1918, its population was about 80 percent Muslim, 10 percent Christian, and 10 percent Jewish. However, rising anti-Semitism in Germany and immigration restrictions in the United States and other countries increased Jewish immigration to Palestine. Arab Palestinians became concerned that the growing Jewish population threatened their dreams of self-rule and formed Muslim-Christian associations to protect their interests.

Throughout the 1920s and 1930s, Palestinian Arab nationalist organizations strongly opposed the British Mandate and the idea of a Jewish homeland in Palestine and argued instead for Arab self-rule. Although the British had some sympathy for their aspirations, they also felt obligated to honor the Balfour Declaration. As a result, many Palestinian Arabs came to regard Jews as foreign invaders who wanted to control them just as the Ottomans and British had.

In contrast, Palestinian Jews believed that a Jewish homeland would provide much-needed sanctuary (safe haven) from the dangers of anti-Semitism. They based their claim on the Bible, which says that God gave the land of Palestine* to Abraham, the father of the Jewish people, about four thousand years ago, and they argued that the Arab claim lacked legitimacy because it was only about fourteen hundred years old. These differences in perspective led to multiple acts of violence during the 1920s and 1930s, killing hundreds on both sides. In 1939, Britain limited Jewish immigration to Palestine in an effort to appease Arab Palestinians about expanding Jewish settlement.

* | In Biblical times, Palestine was called the land of Canaan.

Jewish Refugees: At the same time, rising anti-Semitism in Germany convinced many German Jews to apply for asylum abroad.

When Germany annexed Austria in March 1938 (see above), its 185,000 Jews, like those in Germany, were targeted for deportation, enslavement and death. In July, delegates from thirty-two countries met in New York to discuss the growing number of Jewish refugees, but only the Dominican Republic agreed to accept them*.

> * A few months later, Bolivia also offered to accept some Jews.

In 1939, 900 Jews sailed from Germany to Cuba on the *St. Louis*, a luxury ocean liner. Their plan was to travel from Cuba, which had granted them visas, to the United States, where they hoped to gain asylum. However, Cuba revoked their visas and forced them to leave. The ship then sailed near Florida, but the United States only issued a statement that they, like all immigrants, had to follow the rules and wait their turn. The ship was forced to return to Germany, and although most of its passengers eventually found sanctuary in other countries, 254 of them became victims of the Holocaust.

The misadventures of the *St. Louis* focused international attention on the plight of German Jews, but most countries still refused to accept them. When the British also closed Palestine to Jewish refugees, Jewish groups began smuggling refugees into Palestine and committing terrorist acts against the British. After the war ended and the atrocities of the Holocaust became widely known, the Zionist message that Jews would never be safe until they had a nation of their own persuaded many people and nations to support the Zionist quest for a Jewish homeland.

After the war ended, the United Nations planned to partition Palestine into two states: Israel for Jews and Palestine for Arabs. However, they divided the land equally, upsetting the Arabs, who constituted about two-thirds of the population and argued that the size of their nation should reflect that fact. They began attacking Jewish cities and settlements. Jewish groups fought back and both sides committed atrocities, creating rising tensions throughout the region.

In 1945, Egypt, Syria, Lebanon, Iraq, Transjordan*, Saudi Arabia, and Yemen formed the **Arab League**. In addition to supporting cooperation in building the region's economy, health care, and educational infrastructures, it supported Arab nationalist movements and opposed the creation of a Jewish homeland in Palestine.

* Transjordan changed its name to Jordan in 1946.

First Arab-Israeli War: On **May 14, 1948**, three important things happened. First, the British Mandate's authority over Palestine ended. Second, Israel declared its independence. Third, the Arab League's all-volunteer **Arab Liberation Army** bombed the Jewish city of Tel Aviv. The next day, Israel was invaded by Lebanon, Syria, Egypt, and Iraq, who wanted to support the Palestinian Arabs and express an Arab identity that took precedence over all national or ethnic boundaries. In 1949, the warring nations agreed to an armistice (truce) that included dividing Jerusalem into Jordanian-controlled East Jerusalem and Israeli-controlled West Jerusalem. Over a quarter million Arabs fled or were forced from their homes, and this diaspora (the dispersion of a people from its homeland) created a refugee crisis that remains unresolved today.

The Six-Day War: In May 1967, the leaders of Egypt, Syria, and Jordan began boasting that they would soon invade and defeat

Israel, partly because they believed Soviet misinformation that Israel was planning to attack them. Egyptian radio announced, "All Egypt is now prepared to plunge into total war which will put an end to Israel."

On June 5, 1967, Israel responded to military preparations in Egypt, Syria, and Jordan by destroying the Egyptian air force while it was still on the ground. It followed this surprise strike by sending ground troops into all three countries. In just six days that gave the war its name, Israel captured **Gaza** and the **Sinai** from Egypt, **East Jerusalem** and the **West Bank** from Jordan, and the **Golan Heights** from Syria. The Israelis had about eight hundred casualties, whereas the Arabs suffered approximately twenty thousand.

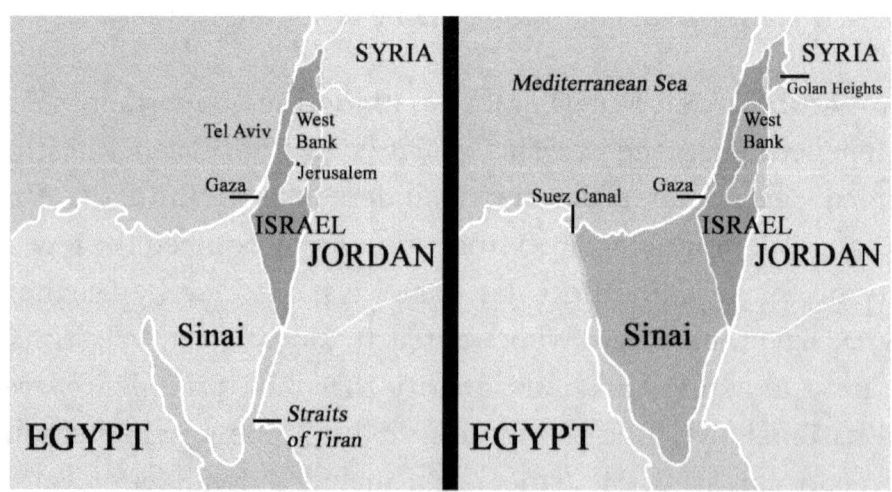

Israel tripled in size and became easier to defend after winning the 1967 Six-Day War.

As Jews celebrated the reunification of Jerusalem after a two-thousand-year exile*, the Arab world struggled with the humiliation of defeat. Approximately one million Arabs lived in the land that Israel seized during the Six-Day War, and hundreds of thousands fled, worsening the refugee crisis that had begun with Israeli independence in 1948.

* Ever since the first-century Roman conquest and expulsion of Jewish residents.

In August 1968, members of the Arab League met in **Khartoum, Sudan,** and issued the **Khartoum Resolution.** This document affirmed Arab unity against Israel's presence in the territories they had just occupied two months earlier and said that Arab League members agreed to the "main principles by which the Arab States abide, namely no peace with Israel, no recognition of Israel, no negotiations with it, and insistence on the rights of the Palestinian people in their own country."

Fourth Arab-Israeli War* (October 1973): This war took place during the Muslim holy month of Ramadan. In an effort to re-take the territory lost in the Six-Day War, Egypt and Syria sent forces across 1967 cease-fire lines on Yom Kippur, the holiest day of the Jewish year. Israel was taken by surprise, and its military was unprepared to fend off an attack. After several days of heavy losses, however, Israel repelled both attacks and drove the invaders to within miles of their own capital cities, Cairo and Damascus.

* Jews call this war the **Yom Kippur War,** and Muslims refer to it as the **Ramadan War.**

Camp David* Accords: Despite Egypt's losses in the Fourth Arab-Israeli war, its president, **Anwar Sadat,** was celebrated because his surprise attack proved that the Israeli army was not invincible (unbeatable). The war shook Israel's confidence in its ability to defend itself and made it willing to negotiate with Egypt. In 1978, President Jimmy Carter** hosted the negotiations at Camp David and played a central role in the accord. Sadat and Israeli Prime Minister **Menachem Begin** signed an historic agreement that has provided a foundation for peace in the Middle East. Egypt regained control of the Sinai Peninsula in exchange for becoming the first Arab nation to recognize Israeli statehood. Begin and Sadat were jointly awarded the 1978 Nobel*** Peace Prize. Two years later, Sadat was assassinated for his participation in the Camp David Accords. References to Sadat, Begin, and the Camp David Accords have appeared at least once on SAT WRITING.

> * | Camp David is a Maryland retreat that is often used to host foreign leaders.

> ** | At least one of President Carter's speeches was used as an essay prompt back when there still was an SAT ESSAY. Therefore, it's quite possible that they could also turn up on SAT READING.

> *** | **Alfred Nobel**, the Swedish chemist who invented **dynamite**, was known as the "Angel of Death" during his lifetime, but his will designated money to create a foundation that would award one prize in each of six categories: chemistry, physics, physiology (medicine), literature, economics, and peace.

The Cold War (1947–1991)

The Cold War is called a "cold" war because its two main adversaries, the United States and the Soviet Union, never engaged each other in actual battle or "hot" fighting. They did, however, participate in **proxy wars*** in many previously colonized countries, and these conflicts resulted in eleven million deaths worldwide. The two superpowers financed and provided military support for their preferred sides in these struggles. As a result, the United States sometimes supported authoritarian leaders who oppressed their own people.

> * A proxy war is fought in a weak country that serves as the battlefield for a conflict between two more powerful countries. Over thirty proxy wars took place around the world during the Cold War, and they were often catastrophic (disastrous) for the people in those countries.

At the end of World War II, the United States felt obligated to help Europe recover economically. In the case of France, this meant helping it keep control over its rebellious colonies in **In-dochina** (southeast Asia). This contradiction between what the United States stood for—human rights, self-determination and democracy—took on racial overtones when the white power structure of the United States sided with white colonizers instead of with their black and brown colonists.

Cold War Basics: Nine American presidents—both Democrat and Republican—held office during the Cold War: **Harry S Truman, Dwight D. Eisenhower, John F. Kennedy, Lyndon B. Johnson, Richard Nixon, Gerald Ford, Jimmy Carter, Ronald Reagan,** and **George H. W. Bush.** All of them made speeches about the nuclear weapons race, the threat that the Soviet Union posed to human rights, and the differences between communist and capitalist economies. These speeches have appeared on SAT READING.

The Soviet leaders during the Cold War were **Joseph Stalin, Nikita Khrushchev, Leonid Brezhnev, Yuri Andropov, Kon-**

stantin Chernenko, and **Mikhail Gorbachev.** Their speeches will almost certainly not appear on the **SAT**, but you should know their names because writers who write about the Cold War may use them as synonyms for the periods in which they held power.

The Soviet Union was a totalitarian communist regime in which every person was (at least theoretically) guaranteed a home, food, and a job. Healthcare and education were provided by the government for free. However, there was no freedom of speech, freedom of the press, or freedom of religion. Women had equal rights, and many became doctors and scientists. Education was provided and controlled by the state, so every student learned the same thing. Atheism (disbelief in the existence of God) was taught in school, and the land and property of churches, synagogues, and mosques were confiscated by the state. People were encouraged to conform with approved norms of behavior, and any perceived opposition to government policies could result in arrest, deportation to a forced labor camp, or death. Soviet conformity is often compared to American freedoms in **SAT READING** passages by writers such as **Eleanor Roosevelt, Winston Churchill**, and **George Orwell.**

Under Stalin, who served as Soviet leader from 1924–1953, the Soviet Union brutally suppressed all opposition. Historians estimate that over twenty million people died as a result of Stalin's policies, many of them in a two-year famine in which between six and eight million people starved to death because of failed collectivized (forced communal) farming projects. Another five to eight million were deliberately murdered. Stalin forcibly relocated entire minority groups thousands of miles to less desirable areas. Millions toiled in labor camps in Siberia. His oppression of Jews, Muslims, and ethnic minorities was especially harsh.

In contrast, the United States is a capitalist democracy in which private individuals engage in economic activity for their own gain. There is freedom of speech, freedom of the press, and freedom of religion. The economy is based on private enterprise, and public education is not based on a federally mandated curriculum. Health care is not currently treated as a human right. Our politics are divisive and complex because multiple viewpoints are represented. Minorities still struggle for justice and dignity. People elect new leaders when they want change, and our government's respect for their choice is shown by a peaceful transfer of power from one leader to the next.*

> *   The only exception was the Capitol Riot on January 6, 2021. However, the riot will probably not be on the SAT because it is recent, unresolved, and controversial.

The Iron Curtain Falls: The "Iron Curtain" is Winston Churchill's metaphorical term for the political and ideological differences between the Soviet Union and the western democratic nations. He first used it in a 1946 speech, arguing that the Soviet Union had drawn an "iron curtain" across Eastern Europe and deprived millions of their basic human rights: freedom of speech, freedom of religion, and freedom to own property. Churchill said that the democratic nations must defend themselves against Soviet expansionism (policy of territorial or economic expansion) and communist ideology. Selections from this speech have appeared on SAT READING.

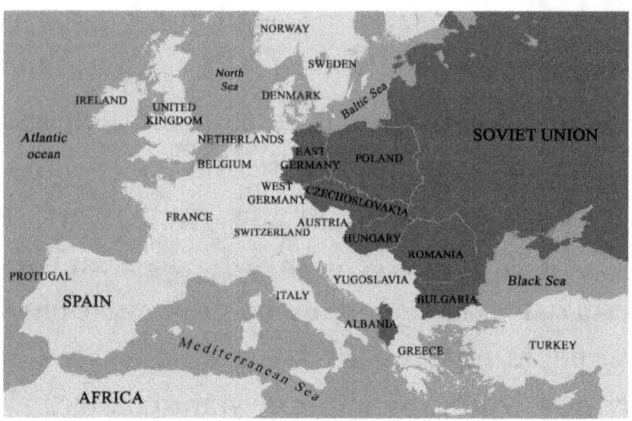

Western Europe was dwarfed by the Soviet
Union during the Cold War.

Eleanor Roosevelt (1884–1962): Winston Churchill wasn't the only leader to worry about the Soviet Union. Eleanor Roosevelt, Franklin Roosevelt's wife, earned respect as first lady during her husband's presidency because she was an outspoken advocate for racial equality, women's rights, education, and the poor. From 1936–1962, she wrote six articles a week for her newspaper column, "My Day." After World War II ended, President Truman appointed her to be the United States' delegate to the United Nations. She helped write the **Universal Declaration of Human Rights** and gave what is probably her most famous speech, "The Struggle for Human Rights," in 1948. In it, she reminds her audience that large numbers of people have been deprived of their human rights by the Soviet Union. Both this speech and articles from her newspaper column have been used as **SAT READING** passages.

Containment*: In 1945, Stalin wanted Poland, Czechoslovakia, Hungary, and Bulgaria to form a Soviet-controlled "buffer zone" to ensure that Russia, which lost between eight and twenty million troops in the war, would never be invaded again. To accomplish this goal, Soviet troops established communist governments in all the countries they "liberated" from the Nazis and eliminated all opposition to Soviet policies. The United States adopted a policy of **containment** to prevent the Soviet Union growing any larger and prevent the spread of communism further into Europe and Asia.

＊ | Holding back.

Truman Doctrine: In 1947, United States President Truman gave a speech in which he argued that the United States should help other countries resist communist takeovers. The Truman Doctrine was a radical break from the isolationism that the United States had embraced before and after World War I, and it set the course of American foreign policy for decades to come. Sections from this speech have been used on SAT READING.

Domino Theory: The domino theory was the belief that if one country in a region such as Asia "fell" to communism, its neighbors would follow suit, the way a row of dominos falls down after just one is knocked over. It was used to justify the United States' involvement in numerous revolutions and assassinations that propelled American-friendly governments into power in the Middle East, Asia, and the Americas.

The domino theory provided an image for what the United States thought would happen if more countries became communist.

Marshall Plan (1948–1952): The Marshall Plan was an important part of the American containment strategy. Named for its creator, **General George C. Marshall**, the plan dedicated more than fifteen billion dollars to rebuild European cities, infrastructure, and industry that had been destroyed during the war. This assistance was seen as an important bulwark (defense) against Soviet efforts to expand communist control of European nations. President Truman's Marshall Plan Speech focuses on the United States' commitment to rebuild Europe and has been used on SAT READING.

Berlin Airlift: The four victorious World War II allies divided Germany into four zones, one each for the Soviets, the Americans, the British, and the French. They did the same with Berlin, the German capital, even though it was deep within the Soviet zone. In early 1948, the British and Americans introduced a new currency as a way to control West Berlin's economy. In June, the Soviets retaliated (fought back) by issuing new East German currency and barricading (blocking) all roads, bridges, and canals that connected West Berlin to the outside world in order to deny its inhabitants of food, coal, and electricity. The United States and Great Britain responded by airlifting (flying) over two million tons of supplies to people in the three besieged sectors of Berlin. As a result, the blockade failed, and the Soviets discontinued it.

North Atlantic Treaty Organization (NATO): In 1949, the United States, Canada, and ten European countries* founded NATO, a mutual defense association intended to stand politically and militarily against Soviet efforts to spread communism in

Western Europe. Like the Marshall Plan, it was an important piece of the United States' strategy of containment.

> * Belgium, Denmark, France, Iceland, Italy, Luxembourg, the Netherlands, Norway, Portugal, and the United Kingdom. Today, NATO includes thirty countries.

In response, the Soviet Union and seven eastern European countries* signed the **Warsaw Pact**. Although they claimed that the Pact was merely (only) a defensive treaty, it alarmed the NATO nations because it gave the Soviet Union control over its members' armies.

> * Albania, Poland, Romania, Hungary, East Germany, Czechoslovakia, and Bulgaria.

Nuclear Arms Race: In 1949, the Soviet Union exploded an atomic bomb at a testing site in Kazakhstan. Suddenly, the United States no longer had a monopoly on nuclear power. Many Americans feared that a nuclear attack by the Soviet Union was (about to happen). The government believed the only defense was to build a nuclear arsenal large enough to convince the Soviets of "**mutual assured destruction (MAD)**," which meant that both sides would be destroyed if either of them started a nuclear war.

By 1950, the United States had 299 nuclear bombs. The Soviet Union had 5 bombs. By 1960, the United States had over 18,000 bombs, and the Soviets had about 200 bombs. Despite this clear numerical advantage, many Americans continued to expect a nuclear attack at any moment. People built bomb shelters that they could live in for weeks if necessary.

Second Red Scare (1947–1957): Following the first Red Scare in the 1920s (above), the United States government constructed a network of agencies that uncovered numerous instances in which American citizens accepted money to spy for the Soviet Union. In 1938, the **House (of Representatives) Committee on Un-American Activities (HUAC)** was established to investigate any citizen or organization suspected of having communist sympathies (feelings).

In 1950, **Senator Joseph McCarthy** claimed to have a list of over two hundred communists and communist sympathizers (supporters). He became the public face of the government's anti-communist campaign, so much so that the term **"McCarthyism"** became synonymous with the second Red Scare. It also became a negative term because he made many false allegations (claims) when accusing people of being communist or having communist associates. These "smear tactics" tarnished his reputation but did nothing to repair the careers and reputations of his targets. Both McCarthy and HUAC were widely criticized for being anti-Semitic because so many Jews were investigated. This era is also known as the **Lavender Scare** because so many LGBTQ+ people—whose sexual identities were often carefully hidden from public view—were suspected of being potential national security risks because their need to hide their sexuality was believed to make them susceptible (likely to give in) to blackmail.

A protest against Lavender Scare policies.

Passages by and about Senator McCarthy have appeared as SAT READING passages. A speech by McCarthy will probably be from the beginning or middle of his career—before he got into trouble—but an SAT WRITING passage about him is more likely going to be from its end.

If you have read **Arthur Miller's** play, *The Crucible*, you probably learned that Miller intended his portrayal of the Salem Witch Trials to be construed (understood) as a critique of McCarthyism; we get the term "witch hunt" from the similarities between the witch trials and HUAC hearings. Shortly after the play was first performed, Miller was subpoenaed (ordered to appear in court) by HUAC. When he refused to provide the committee with new names to investigate, he was jailed, fined, blacklisted*, and forbidden to leave the country.

* | Placed on a list of people not to hire.

Military–Industrial Complex: Although the United States initially reduced the size of its armed forces after the end of World War II, Cold War tensions and the "hot" Korean War* caused it to reverse course, and the American military actually grew throughout the 1950s. The defense industry also grew because it had to supply the growing military and because of the nuclear arms race (above). This combination of the military and the defense industry was called **"the military–industrial complex,"** and President Eisenhower's final speech to the nation warned against allowing it to become too powerful because he feared that it could ultimately threaten democracy. This speech has been used as an SAT READING PASSAGE.

* The combatants (fighting countries) in the Korean War were North Korea and South Korea. The United States did not declare war on North Korea, although Congress authorized President Truman's request to extend the military draft and call up military reservists.

Berlin Wall: A wire fence divided Berlin into Soviet-controlled East Berlin and Allied-controlled West Berlin. However, the fence was easily cut or climbed, and over 2.5 million East Germans escaped into West Berlin between 1949 and 1961. Their departure posed a serious economic threat to East Germany.

On the morning of August 13, 1961, Berliners (people who live in Berlin) awoke to find that a barrier made of barbed wire now completely encircled West Berlin. In the following weeks, roads that connected West Berlin to East Germany were destroyed. Within the city, streets, blocks, and even homes were divided into East and West as residents were barred from parts of their own property. People were separated from families and friends. In the end, a fifteen-foot-tall concrete wall, topped with barbed wire and guarded by armed soldiers in watchtowers divided West Berlin from East Berlin. Not surprisingly, the flood of fleeing East Germans slowed to a trickle. It seemed to many that Winston Churchill's metaphorical "Iron Curtain" (above) had become a hard, physical reality.

Germany 1945-90

Berlin's location deep within the East German Republic made it an attractive goal for East Germans who wanted to flee to the west.

Nonaligned Nations: In 1961, the leaders of Yugoslavia, Egypt, India, Ghana, and Indonesia formed the **Nonaligned Movement** to promote a strong national identity and the right of developing nations to remain uninvolved in the Cold War. Today, the Nonaligned Movement has 120 member countries and remains committed to advocating against all forms of imperial domination.

Space Race: In 1957, the Soviet Union launched *Sputnik I*, the first man-made satellite to orbit Earth. The United States became concerned that the Soviets could be planning to launch a nuclear attack from space and accelerated its own space exploration program in response. The United States also created the **National Aeronautics and Space Administration (NASA)**. President

Kennedy's speeches about the Space Race have frequently appeared on SAT READING.

SAT WRITING also uses passages about the Space Race, so here is a summary of some historical highlights. Explorer I, the first United States satellite, was launched in 1958. In 1959, the Soviet Union landed a space probe on the moon. In 1960, the United States launched the first weather satellite and the first spy satellite. This satellite could take pictures of the Soviet Union and transmit them to the United States. In April 1961, cosmonaut (Soviet astronaut) Yuri Gagarin became the first person to orbit the earth.

One month after Gargarin's space flight, President Kennedy announced that beating the Soviet Union to a moon landing was a national priority. The Apollo Mission first sent unmanned flights into orbit around the Earth in 1966, and on July 20, 1969, American astronauts Buzz Aldrin and Neil Armstrong became the first people ever to set foot on the moon.

The Cuban Revolution: In 1959, Fidel Castro, a communist revolutionary, launched a successful rebellion against the Cuban dictator, General Fulgencio Batista. The United States supported Batista's military dictatorship because it saw Cuba as contested territory in the war against communism. Castro was pro-Soviet and opposed Batista's pro-American policies. Cuban elites and those with ties to Batista's regime fled the country, many to the United States.

Cuba is only about one hundred miles from Florida, and the United States was concerned that the Soviet Union would use

Cuba to gain a foothold in Central America and possibly launch an invasion of the United States.

Bay of Pigs Invasion (April 1961): By the time President Kennedy took office in early 1961, the **United States Central Intelligence Agency (CIA)*** had begun secretly training a group of about fourteen hundred Cuban exiles in Guatemala to invade Cuba and destabilize Castro's regime. The organizers of the attack believed that once the invaders landed, the Cuban people would rise up against the communist government and support a new American-approved leader. However, news of the plan leaked out, and Castro's government had months to prepare in order to defend itself. When the invasion occurred, Castro had a force of twenty thousand soldiers waiting to repel it. In the end, one hundred Americans died, and about twelve thousand invaders surrendered to Cuban forces.

> * The CIA operates intelligence-gathering operations and other covert missions outside of the United States. The Federal Bureau of Investigation (FBI) works within the United States to collect intelligence and to fight domestic terrorism and other federal-level crimes.

President Kennedy was widely criticized for the failed Bay of Pigs invasion. Determined not to appear weak, he authorized **Operation Mongoose**, a complex series of covert CIA actions in Cuba that included several failed plots to assassinate Castro*.

* In 1975, the Senate authorized the **Church Commission** to conduct hearings into Operation Mongoose and similar CIA programs in other countries. Its final report led to widespread condemnation of the CIA for plotting to assassinate Castro and other leaders that the United States opposed.

Cuban Missile Crisis (October 1962): The United States had nuclear-armed missiles on military bases in Turkey that were aimed at the Soviet Union. In response, Soviet leader Nikita Khrushchev secretly placed nuclear-armed missiles in Cuba, close enough to attack the United States. When an American spy plane spotted the missiles, President Kennedy ordered a naval blockade of Cuba. Tensions rose when Soviet ships arrived, and the world waited to see if a nuclear war was about to begin. After several days of secret negotiations, the Soviet Union agreed to remove the missiles from Cuba on condition that the United States also removed its nuclear missiles from Turkey. Kennedy also promised that the United States would not invade Cuba again.

After the Cuban Missile Crisis was resolved, the leaders of both superpowers realized how close their countries had come to mutual destruction. As a result, they established a direct telephone line between the White House and the **Kremlin** (the Soviet government's main location). They also began negotiating a series of agreements that were designed to limit the number of nuclear weapons each side possessed and ban aboveground tests of nuclear bombs.

Assassination of President Kennedy (November 22, 1963): President Kennedy was assassinated in Dallas, Texas, on November 22,

1963. His assassin, **Lee Harvey Oswald**, also killed a Dallas police officer before being apprehended (arrested) in a movie theater. However, Oswald himself was assassinated while in police custody, and his assassin, **Jack Ruby**, died in prison while waiting to appeal his death sentence for shooting Oswald. All of this led to many theories about what "really" happened. The government's **Warren Commission** concluded that Oswald acted alone when he shot Kennedy and that Ruby acted alone when he shot Oswald. However, many people remained unconvinced and claimed that Fidel Castro or the American CIA was behind the assassination of the president. Many books and movies have explored these theories, and some people still believe them today.

Vice President Lyndon Baines Johnson (LBJ) was sworn in as president on Air Force One less than two hours after President Kennedy was pronounced dead.

Despite President Kennedy's short time in office, his legacy as an inspiring leader remains strong, and many of his speeches on the Cold War, civil rights and the exploration of space have been used as SAT READING passages.

Chinese Communist Revolution (1949): When the Japanese invaded China in 1937 (above), they interrupted a long civil war between the Kuomintang (KMT), led by **Chiang Kai-shek**, and the Communist Party of China, led by **Mao Zedong**. After World War II ended, the civil war resumed, but now the conflict had new implications. When Mao announced the creation of the communist **People's Republic of China**, he joined the Soviet quest to spread communism around the world. The Sino-Soviet (Chinese-Soviet) alliance fueled the Cold War in Asia because China shares borders with fourteen other countries*. Five of these—Kazakhstan, Kyrgyzstan, Laos, North Korea, and Tajikistan—were already communist. According to the domino theory (above) this meant the other countries were in danger of "falling" to communism as well.

> *   Afghanistan, Bhutan, India, Kazakhstan, North Korea, Kyrgyzstan, Laos, Mongolia, Burma (renamed Myanmar in 1989), Nepal, Pakistan, Russia, Tajikistan, and Vietnam. China also shares maritime (ocean) borders with Brunei, Indonesia, Japan, South Korea, Malaysia, the Philippines, and Taiwan.

The Korean War (1950–1953): The Korean War was the Cold War's first proxy war. It is sometimes called the "**Forgotten War**" because it seemed insignificant (unimportant) after the enormity (large size) of World War II.

After Japan surrendered in 1945, the Allies divided Korea into two zones at the thirty-eighth parallel*, a latitude (imaginary line marking distance from the equator) that cuts through the center of the country. Japanese troops to the north of this line surrendered to the Soviet Union, those south of the line surrendered to Allied forces.

> * References to the thirty-eighth parallel are generally references to the Korean War.

In 1948, **North Korea** became a socialist country led by **Kim Il-sung**, the grandfather of today's leader, **Kim Jong-un**. At the same time, **South Korea** became an independent capitalist country headed by **Syngman Rhee**. Both men were ruthless authoritarian leaders. North Korea was financially and militarily supported by China and the Soviet Union, and South Korea received money and military aid from the United Nations and the United States.

In 1950, North Korean troops, backed by China and the Soviet Union, invaded South Korea. The United States joined the war on South Korea's side a few months later, and Americans' fear of communism intensified. By the time the fighting ended in 1953, about five million people had died. Korea remains divided into North and South today.

The Vietnam War (1955–1975): Vietnam became a French colony* in the 1840s. Its independence movement began almost immediately. In 1919, **Ho Chi Minh**, a Vietnamese activist and committed socialist, traveled to Versailles specifically to meet with President Woodrow Wilson. He wanted American support for his people's efforts to free their country from French rule and believed that the United States' revolutionary history and commitment to self-government made it a natural ally of the Vietnamese people. However, he was disappointed. President Wilson valued the United States' alliance with France too much to support its colonists' desire for independence. This was a mistake. Ho Chi Minh quickly learned that the Soviet Union was extremely willing to assist his country's quest for freedom.

* The French called Vietnam "Indochine," or Indochina.

In 1950, the United States began sending advisors to help the French control their colony. Even so, Vietnamese forces won a decisive victory against the French in 1954. Like North Korea, **North Vietnam** became an independent communist country. Throughout the 1950s and 1960s, the United States supported an anti-communist government in **South Vietnam**, despite increasingly clear evidence that it was corrupt, incompetent, and unpopular.

President Kennedy more than doubled the United States' economic and military support of the South Vietnamese regime and increased the number of American military advisers from seven hundred to over sixteen thousand. However, these investments did not reform the South Vietnamese government or make it any more able to govern, and its president was killed in a military coup in November 1963.

When President Kennedy was assassinated about three weeks later, Vice President **Lyndon B. Johnson** became president. Johnson was a decorated World War II veteran, an experienced politician, and a longtime advocate for the poor. As president, Johnson pursued his vision of a "Great Society," his name for a country that had freed its citizens from poverty and racial injustice. He supported government programs designed to improve education and health care and to alleviate (lessen) both rural and urban poverty. He signed the Civil Rights Act, the Voting Rights Act, and the Immigration and Nationality Act, which prohibited discrimination based on national origin, race or ancestry and reversed decades of race-based immigration quotas.

Gulf of Tonkin (August 1964): President Johnson was also committed to winning the Cold War. He ignored State Department reports that the situation in South Vietnam was deteriorating and began searching for ways to escalate American involvement as soon as he took office. A report of unprovoked attacks* on two American destroyer-class war-ships in the Gulf of Tonkin prompted Congress to pass the Gulf of Tonkin Resolution, giving President Lyndon B. Johnson permission to wage open war in Vietnam.

* The report Congress heard was not entirely true. Only one destroyer was attacked, and it was spying for the South Vietnamese. In 1971, classified (secret) military documents suggested Johnson had lied to Congress about the attacks in order to win support to escalate the war in Vietnam. This suspicion was confirmed in 2005 when additional documents were legally declassified (declared no longer secret).

Johnson's escalation of the war in Vietnam drained resources from "Great Society" programs, which stalled as a result. By the time he left office in 1968, President Johnson, whose nickname was LBJ, was deeply unpopular for his handling of the war. Even his long-time ally Martin Luther King, Jr., made a speech in which he denounced the war as an attack on the poor. This speech was used as a prompt for the now-defunct (dead) SAT ESSAY, which suggests that it could also be a candidate for an SAT READING passage.

A popular anti-war chant was "Hey, hey, LBJ, how many kids did you kill today?" In 1965, Johnson sent the first combat troops to South Vietnam, and the conflict escalated significantly.

President Johnson inherited the worsening situation in Vietnam. The United States government saw the Vietnam War as a high-stakes **Cold War** conflict. When its assumptions about the situation in Vietnam did not lead to the expected victories, it increasingly relied on tactics that were justified by the domino theory (above) and kept secrets from the American public. As you'll see, some of those secret strategies led to war crimes and atrocities that undermined Americans' confidence in their government when they came to light.

The Vietnam War was the first televised war. When discrepancies (differences) occurred between government statements about the war and news by on-the-ground reporters in Vietnam, many Americans became convinced that the war was illegal, immoral, and inconsistent with American values. Images of violence by American soldiers in the news media and stories of mass killings, rape, and torture helped create opposition to the war and led people to question its stated purpose.

Operation Rolling Thunder (1964–1973): Using the war powers granted by the Gulf of Tonkin Resolution, President Johnson authorized **Operation Rolling Thunder**, which ultimately dropped more than three million bombs on the **Ho Chi Minh Trail***—more than all the bombs used during World War II. The bombs killed civilians and destroyed people's homes and livelihoods, increasing support throughout Vietnam for the North Vietnamese. Today, the bombing campaign is generally seen as a mistake and cited as an example of why bombing campaigns do not win wars without the support of ground troops.

> *   A north-south military supply route that was over nine hundred miles long. The North Vietnamese built it to transport people, weapons, and other supplies to and from South Vietnam.

Tet Offensive (January 1968): By the end of 1967, the Vietnam War had become a stalemate. The North Vietnamese government launched the **Tet Offensive** by attacking thirteen South Vietnamese cities. Although the attacks did not persuade South Vietnamese people to ally with the North, the Tet Offensive was an important strategic victory that allowed the North Vietnamese to remain on the offensive for the rest of the war. In response, the United States escalated its commitment to South Vietnam by sending 200,000 additional troops to fight alongside the South Vietnamese.

My Lai Massacre (1968): The village of My Lai was believed to be harboring (hiding) **Vietcong*** soldiers, so a company of American soldiers was sent to capture them. There were no Vietcong present when they arrived, but the soldiers massacred about

504 villagers, including 17 pregnant women and 173 children, 56 of whom were infants. Many of the women were raped before they were killed. The massacre was covered up by US Army officials for a year before it was finally reported. In response to worldwide outrage, the army conducted an investigation and recommended the indictment of 28 officers. When only 14 were tried and only one received a significant prison sentence, it contributed to the low morale of the American forces.

* | South Vietnamese guerillas who supported North Vietnam.

Tallying the Dead: Although the conflict in Vietnam intensified, it remained a stalemate. Battles were fought, but it was often impossible to tell whether any strategic or military objective had been achieved. As a result, reporting on the war's progress became a matter of tallying (counting) the numbers of people **killed in action (KIA)** for each side. Americans responded to daily KIA reports in the news by questioning whether the war was really about defending democracy in Vietnam or if it were merely a proxy in the Cold War against the Soviet Union.

Nixon's Vietnam Policy: President Nixon pursued *détente*, a policy of easing Cold War tensions with the Soviet Union and China. He hoped that warming relationships would help the United States leave Vietnam "with honor" because it had become increasingly clear that the United States could not win a lasting victory in Vietnam.

Near the end of 1969, Nixon announced that his administration was preparing to leave Vietnam by gradually withdrawing American troops while also arming and training the South Vietnamese army to fight on its own. He called this process "Vietnamizing the war" and asked "the great silent majority of my fellow Americans" for their support as he sought "to end the war in a way that we could win the peace."

At first, Nixon tried to negotiate with North Vietnam to end the war. When that failed, however, he secretly authorized bombing neutral Cambodia because portions of the Ho Chi Minh trail ran through it and into Laos, which the United States had been bombing since 1964. In 1970, American ground troops invaded Cambodia, hoping to destroy North Vietnamese bases and disrupt their supply lines. When Nixon announced the incursion (invasion), there were protests on college campuses throughout the United States. At Ohio's **Kent State University**, four student protestors were killed, and nine others were wounded when some members of the National Guard fired into the crowd. Less than two weeks later, two students were killed and twelve injured in a similar incident at the historically black **Jackson State University** in Mississippi.

Pentagon Papers: In 1971, a military analyst shared a number of secret government documents about the Vietnam War with several major American newspapers. They revealed the covert (secret) bombing of Laos and Cambodia as well as a number of other attacks that had not been reported in American media. The information increased the opposition to the war. When the Nixon administration tried to block their publication, the Supreme Court ruled that the government did not have a compelling argument for interfering with the First Amendment rights of a free press. Two recent movies, *The Post* and *The Pentagon Papers*, portray these events.

Nixon Goes to China: In 1972, President Nixon became the first American president to visit the People's Republic of China. The trip was an international success because it began the process of easing relations with China and showed that Nixon had softened his approach to the Cold War.

A few months later, Nixon also traveled to the Soviet Union, where he and Soviet leader **Leonid Brezhnev** concluded the **Strategic Arms Limitation Talks (SALT) Treaty** to limit their nuclear arsenals (collections). The agreement eased tensions between the two superpowers and gave Nixon a foreign policy victory during his 1972 reelection campaign.

Watergate Scandal: In the summer of 1972, five employees of President Nixon's reelection campaign were caught breaking into the Democratic Party headquarters in the **Watergate Hotel's** complex of office buildings. It was their second break-in; a month earlier, they had photographed Democratic campaign documents and bugged (hacked) their office telephones. President Nixon denied all knowledge of the burglaries and won reelection in November.

Listening devices were placed in the handsets
of Democratic Party office telephones.

Two *Washington Post* reporters, **Bob Woodward** and **Carl Bernstein**, uncovered evidence that Nixon had lied. These suspicions were confirmed by an anonymous source known to them only as "**Deep Throat**," as well as by court testimony in which Nixon's own aides alleged that Nixon had secretly tape-recorded Oval Office (the president's office) conversations. For most of 1973, the Nixon administration fought to avoid releasing these tapes, but the Supreme Court ordered him to turn them over to investigators in July 1974. When Nixon still did not turn over the tapes, the **House Judiciary Committee*** voted to impeach (charge with misconduct) him for obstructing (blocking) justice, abusing the power of his office and covering up his involvement in the two Watergate burglaries. Faced by impeachment in the House of Representatives and a trial in the Senate, Nixon resigned from office. **Vice President Gerald Ford** became president, and one of his first acts was to pardon Nixon, although several members of the Nixon administration were tried and jailed.

* This committee is responsible for overseeing federal courts and other government law enforcement agencies.

Fall of Saigon: The Vietnam War ended in 1975, when North Vietnamese troops entered Saigon, the capital of South Vietnam. Most American troops had been withdrawn in 1973, but a force of 7,200 remained to assist the South Vietnamese. As the North Vietnamese took control, refugees, many of whom had worked for the American government, swarmed into Saigon, hoping to be evacuated along with the departing Americans. The United States evacuated thousands of refugees to Guam before it finally airlifted the last Marines from the roof of the American embassy in Saigon.

Cambodian Civil War: Khmer is the Cambodian word for both the Cambodian people and their language. Between 1970 and 1975, the communist guerilla organization **Khmer Rouge** (Red Khmer) and the military government of the **Khmer Republic** engaged in a brutal civil war that left about 10 percent of the country's population dead. The North Vietnamese supported the Khmer Rouge while the United States and South Vietnam backed the Khmer Republic. However, when the United States pulled out of Vietnam in 1973, it also stopped helping the Khmer Republic, which lost to the Khmer Rouge in 1975.

Cambodian Genocide: Between 1975 and 1979, the Khmer Rouge, led by the dictator **Pol Pot**, tried to create a classless communist society. They evacuated the capital city of **Phnom Penh** and forced its population to work on large agricultural projects where many died from inadequate food, disease, and harsh treatment. The Khmer Rouge also executed thousands of educated, middle-class Cambodians because it said they were "enemies of the state." During this period, over two million Cambodians lost their lives. These losses, combined with the half million or so that occurred during the Cambodian Civil War, meant that about 25 percent of Cambodia's population died in less than ten years.

In 1977, the Khmer Rouge began conducting border raids into Vietnam, where they burned entire villages and massacred the inhabitants. In 1979, Vietnam invaded Cambodia, captured Phnom Penh, established a new government, and forced Pol Pot and the Khmer Rouge into the jungles. After this victory, Vietnam established a puppet government in Cambodia and remained as an occupying force for ten years.

Indochina Refugee Crisis: Between 1975 and 2010, three million people fled communist regimes in Vietnam, Laos, and Cambodia, many of them in overcrowded small boats that earned them the nickname **Boat People.** As many as 400,000 may have died at sea. Ultimately, about a million refugees were resettled in the United States in the largest such effort in American history. Excerpts from memoirs and novels about these events have appeared as literature passages on **SAT READING.**

Vietnamese "boat people."

Civil Rights Movements

Many American students think the Civil Rights movement began in the 1950s when **Rosa Parks** was arrested for refusing to move to the back of a segregated bus in Montgomery, Alabama, and **Dr. Martin Luther King, Jr.,** organized the Montgomery bus boycott. However, as you may have realized by now, the events of the 1950s and 1960s, while important, are only a small part of the struggles of African Americans in the United States. The movement began before the Civil War and resumed after Reconstruction ended in 1877 when Black Codes and racial violence began to undermine the newfound freedom of African Americans. It continued through the Great Migration that began in 1916 and both World Wars. It inspired the second wave of the feminist movement, the Native American rights movement, the Chicano rights movement, and the gay rights movement. Today, it exists in the #BlackLivesMatter movement and the efforts to end systemic racial inequality in education, income, health care, and the justice system.

By the 1950s, many African Americans were conviced that American democracy did not include them, despite their honorable service in every war the United States had ever fought. Black soldiers returned from fighting overseas only to discover that they were supposed to go back to being second-class citizens when they returned home. Although some, like **Medgar Evers** (below), were able to take advantage of the government benefits awarded to veterans by the **GI Bill of 1944** to attend college, others faced discrimination based on their race. Black veterans were denied mortgages by local banks or forced into substandard segregated housing.

Brown v. Board of Education (1954): The Supreme Court's 1896 decision in *Plessy v. Ferguson* (above) made segregation the law of the land. The doctrine of "separate but equal" meant that all-black schools received less funding and fewer resources than all-white schools did. Black students often had to use hand-me-down textbooks that white schools had discarded. Sometimes, white students defaced these books with racist insults before sending them to all-black schools.

School desegregation had been a top priority of the **National Association for the Advancement of Colored People (NAACP)** since the 1930s, and it had successfully won lawsuits against segregation in higher education. In 1954, the Supreme Court agreed to review the issue of segregation in public schools by combining five similar cases into one, *Brown v. Board of Education of Topeka, Kansas*. The court ruled that racially segregated public schools were fundamentally unequal and that local school districts must desegregate their schools "at all deliberate speed."

Little Rock Nine: Although many Southern school districts complied with the law, some did not. In September 1957, Arkansas governor **Orval Faubus** activated the **Arkansas National Guard** to prevent nine African American teenagers from attending the all-white **Central High School** in Little Rock, the state capital. Unattractive images of white people screaming at the students, who became known as the **Little Rock Nine**, appeared in newspapers and television news programs. President Eisenhower was concerned about world opinion and angered by what he viewed as Faubus's insubordination (refusal to obey orders), so he federalized (took command of) the Arkansas National Guard and ordered them to protect the **Little Rock Nine** both inside and outside the school building, which they did until May 1958.

Murder of Emmett Till: In 1955, fourteen-year-old **Emmett Till** traveled from his home in Chicago to visit family in Mississippi. When a white woman, Carolyn Bryant, claimed that he had flirted with her in a local store, her husband and her brother kidnapped Till, gouged out his eyes, and beat him to death. They tied his body to the fan of a cotton gin with barbed wire and threw it into the Tallahatchie River. When Till's body was recovered, his mother insisted that his body be returned to Chicago for burial. When she saw how badly mutilated her son was, she insisted on having his coffin open during the funeral so that everyone could see what had been done to him.

In 2017, historian Timothy Tyson wrote that Carolyn Bryant admitted to him that Till never touched or threatened her in any way. Since then, however, members of her family have denied Tyson's claim and kept her location a secret.

Montgomery Bus Boycott (1955–1956): Alabama was a priority for civil rights organizers because **Governor George Wallace** was an outspoken opponent of desegregation. Its capital, Montgomery, became central in the struggle for civil rights when **Rosa Parks** refused to move to the back of a segregated bus in Montgomery and sparked a boycott of the city's bus system.

Parks's story is often presented to students as the spontaneous (unplanned) action of a tired woman. However, that version turns Parks into an accidental hero when she was really an experienced civil rights activist who had worked for the NAACP (above) for over a decade at the time of her arrest. Her refusal to move was part of a much larger campaign for **"transit equity"** (equal access to transportation), and her action was part of a deliberate NAACP strategy to draw attention to the unfairness of racially segregated busing. Her arrest resulted in a 381-day boycott that involved organizing transportation for Montgomery's forty thousand black citizens. This deprived the Montgomery bus company of about 70 percent of its riders and revenue (income).

Dr. Martin Luther King, Jr.: The Montgomery Bus Boycott brought King, a Southern Baptist minister with a PhD in divinity*, into the national spotlight. King believed in Mohandas Gandhi's doctrine of nonviolent protest (above) and compared African Americans' struggle against segregation to the Indian struggle for independence that Gandhi led. King was also a skilled orator (speechmaker) who was famous for his persuasive speeches on civil rights and nonviolence.

> * The Christian study of the relationship between God and humanity.

King was married to **Coretta Scott King** and the couple had four children. During the bus boycott, their home was firebombed. The family escaped, and Dr. King used the occasion to preach about loving one's enemy.

Browder v. Gale (1956): Civil rights activists filed a lawsuit against the bus company on behalf of four passengers who had been ejected from their seats. Six months later, the Supreme Court ruled that Alabama's racial segregation of public transportation was unconstitutional.

After the Montgomery Bus Boycott, King and other civil rights leaders founded the **Southern Christian Leadership Conference (SCLC)** as an umbrella organization to coordinate civil rights activities among various local and state organizations. King served as its president until his assassination in 1968.

Freedom Rides (1961): Although federal law had outlawed segregation on interstate buses, Southern states were determined to maintain it throughout the South. To protest this violation of federal law, an interracial group of civil rights activists chartered two buses from Washington, DC, and traveled south. Buses were firebombed in Anniston, Alabama, and Birmingham. Police commissioner **Eugene "Bull"** Connor allowed Ku Klux Klan members to beat riders with baseball bats and chains. White riders were targeted for especially severe beatings for showing disloyalty to their race. Local hospitals refused to treat injured riders.

When the buses arrived in Jackson, Mississippi, the riders were arrested.

Over four hundred people, many of them from the unsegregated North, participated in about sixty different Freedom Rides, and their commitment gained worldwide support for the Civil Rights Movement.

Images like this one gained international support for the Freedom Riders.

Birmingham Campaign: Martin Luther King, Jr., referred to Birmingham, Alabama, as "the most segregated city in America." Its police force, led by **"Bull" Connor**, responded to peaceful protests with violence. Shocking images of police officers arresting elementary school children and turning fire hoses and attack dogs on protestors appeared in newspapers and television news reports all over the world. As a result, Birmingham became an international symbol of violent racism.

King was arrested during one such protest, and he used his time in jail to write **"Letter from Birmingham Jail"** to respond to the criticisms of white Alabama clergy. In the letter, King says that it's wrong to condemn peaceful protesters for stirring up trouble without also considering why they are protesting in the first place. He also explains that African Americans "know through painful experience that freedom is never voluntarily given by the oppressor; it must be demanded by the oppressed." There are many famous quotes from this letter, which was published in national magazines and Christian newspapers. It created widespread support among white people for both King and the civil rights movement, and it has appeared on SAT READING.

Fire hoses knocked protestors to the ground.

Birmingham Church Bombing: The Birmingham campaign was successful. In May 1963, the city agreed to desegregate its lunch counters, restrooms, and water fountains and to allow black people to work in retail stores. Four months later, white supremacists bombed the all-black 16th Street Baptist Church shortly before Sunday worship services were scheduled to start. Four girls, aged eleven to fourteen, were killed and fourteen others were injured.

Bombs were not new to Birmingham's African American community—the city's nickname was "Bombingham"—and thousands of angry protesters gathered at the crime scene. Governor George Wallace ordered arrests of the protestors, and riots broke out across the city in response. President Kennedy ordered the

National Guard to keep the peace. Even though the perpetrators of the bombing were known to the police and FBI by 1965, it took multiple trials and almost forty years for the first of the four men to be convicted.

March on Washington for Jobs and Freedom (1963): Civil rights activists organized a march in Washington, DC, on the centennial (one-hundred-year anniversary) of the Emancipation Proclamation to highlight how much injustice African Americans still faced. About 250,000 people attended, making it larger than any previous human rights demonstration in the United States. Martin Luther King, Jr. gave his famous **"I Have a Dream"** speech, which could easily appear as an SAT READING passage. The speech says that African Americans are still not free a century after emancipation because they live "on a lonely island of poverty in the midst of a vast ocean of material prosperity." King also says that for black people, the Declaration of Independence is like a "bad check" that has been returned for "insufficient funds" and that "we must rise to the majestic heights of meeting physical force with soul force."

John Lewis: One of the original Freedom Riders, **John Lewis** was badly beaten in Alabama on two separate occasions. He had already been arrested twenty-four times when he was elected as the chairman of the **Student Nonviolent Coordinating Committee (SNCC)**, and he was among the speakers at the March on Washington. In his speech he said that President Kennedy's civil rights bill does not protect African Americans' right to vote strongly enough and that it does not adequately address the country's economic inequality. He also says that black people are "tired" of waiting: "We want our freedom, and we want it now. We do not want to go to jail. But we will go to jail if this is the price we must pay for love, brotherhood and true peace." Lewis later ran for the United States House of Representatives, won, and was reelected sixteen times. He is famous for saying that getting into trouble while working for justice is "good trouble, necessary trouble," a comment that was much quoted in the coverage about his death from cancer in 2020. Any of his speeches could appear on SAT READING.

Murder of Medgar Evers (1963): A veteran of the 1944 invasion of Normandy, Medgar Evers returned to his native Mississippi after the war and became active in the Civil Rights Movement. The first NAACP field officer in the state, Evers participated in desegregating the University of Mississippi. He was conducting an independent investigation of Emmett Till's murder when he began receiving death threats. In the weeks before his death, he survived two attempts on his life before being shot in the back in his driveway. His family convinced a white hospital to treat him (a first in Mississippi), but he died from his wounds anyway. He was buried with full military honors at Arlington National Cemetery, but it took until 1994 for his killer to be convicted for his murder.

Freedom Summer (1964): In Mississippi, less than 10 percent of eligible black voters were registered to vote, so the state was targeted by civil rights organizations for a summer voter registration drive. Hundreds of volunteers, both black and white, traveled to Mississippi. Among them were **James Chaney**, who was black, and two white volunteers, **Michael Schwerner** and **Andrew Goodman**. In June, the three of them were arrested for speeding in Philadelphia, Mississippi, and briefly jailed before being released and escorted out of town by police. They were then taken from their car and murdered by a group that included both Ku Klux Klan members and local police. Their bodies were not found until August. Although there were a number of arrests,

Mississippi officials refused to press charges against anyone until 2005, when one man was convicted; he received a sixty-year sentence and died in prison.

Civil Rights Act of 1964: The March on Washington and Medgar Evers's murder are credited with helping to convince Congress to pass a sweeping civil rights bill that prohibited segregation on the basis of race, color, religion, sex, and national origin in public institutions such as schools. The ruling overturned the 1896 Supreme Court decision in *Plessy v. Ferguson* (above) that made "separate but equal" the law of the land. Dr. King won the 1964 Nobel Peace Prize for his commitment to nonviolent resistance to racial injustice. His acceptance speech could appear on SAT READING.

Selma-to-Montgomery March (1965): The passage of the Civil Rights Act made it illegal to prevent African Americans from voting. However, voter registration workers continued to face hostility and violence from whites throughout the South. The SCLC decided to focus its registration efforts on Selma, Alabama, where only 2 percent of the African American population had been able to register to vote.

Selma is only fifty-four miles from Montgomery, but it took three tries for activists to make the march. On "**Bloody Sunday,**" state and local police used tear gas and billy clubs to drive them back from the **Edmund Pettus Bridge*** before they could leave Selma. John Lewis was hit in the head so hard that his skull cracked. Two days later, Dr. King led a second group to the bridge, where they again were halted by police. This time, no violence occurred. After a federal judge ruled that the right to protest includes the right to use roads and bridges for that purpose, the marchers were finally allowed to leave Selma and march to Montgomery.

This time, the marchers were protected by 3,000 military police and troops. About 3,200 people left Selma, and about 22,000 more joined the marchers along the road to Montgomery. You may have seen the 2014 movie, *Selma*, which depicts the events of Bloody Sunday.

> ✻ Edmund Pettus was a Confederate general, a member of the United States Senate, and a leader of the Alabama Ku Klux Klan. Since the 2020 death of John Lewis, who was one of the leaders of the Selma-to-Montgomery March, there has been an effort to rename the bridge for him.

Voting Rights Act (1965): The murders of Chaney, Schwerner, and Goodman (above) and the violence that took place in Selma created broad support for the **Voting Rights Act**. It outlawed all discriminatory voting practices, such as literacy tests and poll taxes, and said that states that had a history of disenfranchising black voters were subject to federal oversight. Within the first year after the Act's passage, over 250,000 African Americans had registered to vote.

The Voting Rights Act was renewed several times. Section 5 of the law required that states and counties with a record of voter suppression seek permission from the federal court before enacting any new voting legislation. However, in 2013 Shelby County, Alabama, asked the Supreme Court to overturn the requirement for federal oversight on the grounds that the situation in the supervised states and counties had changed since 1965. The Supreme Court agreed, and by 2016 almost nine hundred polling places had closed nationwide, many of them in districts with high numbers of African Americans.

The issue of voting continues to be controversial. As of early 2021 some states have moved to expand access by permitting same-day voter registration, early voting, mail-in voting, and restoring the voting rights of people convicted of felonies. However, others have gone in the opposite direction. Voter ID laws, restrictions on early voting and mail-in voting, and other measures have been passed in some states.

Since these efforts are both ongoing and controversial, they are unlikely to be discussed in an SAT passage. However, they illustrate a central theme of history as it appears on SAT READING, which often features paired passages about voting rights from different moments in American history.

Malcolm X was born Malcolm Little. His childhood was marred (damaged) by white supremacist violence that included his father's murder and his mother's resulting mental breakdown. He dropped out of school after eighth grade because his history teacher told him that black people could not be lawyers. In his early twenties, he was sentenced to jail for his participation in a home burglary ring.

While in prison, Malcolm converted to the **Nation of Islam**, an Islamic black nationalist group whose beliefs combine mainstream Islamic beliefs with a belief in black racial superiority. In 1950, he changed his last name, Little, to X: "For me, my 'X' replaced the white slavemaster name of 'Little' which some blue-eyed devil name Little had imposed upon my paternal forebears." That year, Malcolm also declared that he was a communist in a letter to President Truman in which he expressed his opposition to the Korean War; the letter prompted the FBI to open a file on him.

After his release from prison in 1952, Malcolm began to preach for the Nation of Islam. His message of racial pride and black self-defense appealed to many African Americans who, like him, were frustrated with the slow progress of the civil rights movement. He called Christianity the religion of white colonizers and said that Islam, which arrived in Africa in the eighth century, was a better religion for black people.

Many people—both black and white—found Malcolm X disturbing. In addition to agreeing that black people should defend themselves against white violence, he said they should remain separate from white people whenever possible. He accused white civil rights supporters of hypocrisy (saying one thing and doing another) because of the "white flight" that occurred whenever African Americans tried to buy homes in suburban neighborhoods.

In 1963, Malcolm X went on a pilgrimage (religious journey) to the Muslim holy city of Mecca. He rejected the Nation of Islam's belief in black genetic superiority when he realized that there were Muslims of all races. He began working to build an international human rights coalition. However, his change of philosophy angered the Nation of Islam's leaders. He and his family received death threats and their home was bombed. He was assassinated in early 1965 by a Nation of Islam member who was captured at the scene of the crime and confessed to the shooting.

Student Nonviolent Coordinating Committee (SNCC*): This student group was inspired by the civil rights movement. Its high school and college-aged members participated in sit-ins, voter registration drives, Freedom Rides, and the 1963 March on Washington. In the mid-1960s, many SNCC members became impatient with the pace of nonviolent change and began to advocate more militant approaches.

> * Pronounced "snick."

In June 1966, twenty-four-year-old SNCC Chairman **Stokely Carmichael** was arrested in Greenwood, Mississippi, for his civil rights activism. It was his twenty-seventh arrest for nonviolent protest. After his release he rejected nonviolence in a speech to supporters: "We been saying freedom for six years and we ain't got nothin. What we got to start saying now is Black Power! We want Black Power."

Carmichael's speech popularized the phrase, **"Black Power,"** and it became immediately controversial. Many black people understood it as an affirmation of black pride and self-determination, but many civil rights leaders and white people thought it sounded threatening and anti-white.

Black Power Movement: Black Power activists believed in self-defense against white violence and self-reliance for African American communities. The **Black Panther Party** taught its members to "copwatch" while openly carrying guns, prompting the California legislature to outlaw the public display of weapons. FBI director **J. Edgar Hoover*** called the Black Panthers "the greatest threat to the internal security of the country."

> * Not to be confused with President Herbert Hoover.

Black Power activists also supported economic development in black communities. They created schools, community centers, and political organizations and advocated for the inclusion of African and African American history, culture, and literature in schools and universities. The slogan, "Black is Beautiful," was intended to combat the idea that only white skin, blond hair, and blue eyes were beautiful. It told African American girls and women that they were beautiful and did not need to try to look like white women. Both men and women were encouraged to grow their hair out naturally instead of using chemical or heat treatment to make it look like white people's hair. The "Afro" became a political symbol because it was a visible symbol of African heritage that defied white beauty norms.

Black Power activist **Angela Davis** wore an Afro to symbolize her rejection of white beauty standards. However, she was annoyed when people focused on her hair because she viewed her activism as much more important than her appearance.

1967 Race Riots: During the summer of 1967, 159 race riots took place in American cities. Most of them erupted after police used violence against African American men who were accused of minor offenses. In **Newark, New Jersey,** the beating of a black cab driver by two white police officers sparked six days of riots that destroyed entire sections of the city and left twenty-six people dead. In **Detroit, Michigan,** an even larger riot began when police officers raided an unlicensed bar in the black section of the city. This time, there were forty-three dead, thirty-three of whom were black. In both cities, thousands of National Guard troops were deployed, thousands of people were arrested, hundreds were injured, and millions of dollars in property damage was done.

Assassination of Martin Luther King, Jr.: In 1968, Martin Luther King, Jr. was assassinated in Memphis, Tennessee, where he had been supporting a strike by that city's black sanitation workers. President Lyndon B. Johnson declared a national day of mourning, and King's funeral was attended by thousands. Despite this outpouring of respect for King and his lifetime commitment to civil rights, many African Americans felt that his violent death proved that nonviolence would never succeed against white racism.

Robert F. Kennedy, President Kennedy's younger brother, spoke to a crowd a few hours later. He said that his brother's 1963 assassination had caused him similar pain and that it was important to remember that the goal is for everyone to live together in peace. Two months later, Kennedy, who was competing for the Democratic Party's nomination for president of the United States, was also assassinated. His death left the Democratic Party in chaos and contributed to the victory of Republican **Richard M. Nixon** in the 1968 presidential election.

Second-Wave Feminism: The **Equal Rights Amendment (ERA)** was first introduced in 1923. It reads, "Equality of rights under the law shall not be denied or abridged by the United States or by any State on account of sex." However, only thirty-five of the required thirty-eight states ratified it before the government-set deadline, and the amendment seemed to have been defeated.

Since 2017, however, Nevada, Illinois, and Virginia have ratified the amendment, and a resolution to overrule the deadline has been introduced in Congress. If it is ratified, equal rights for women will become part of the United States Constitution.

Many of the women who worked during World War II were fired from their wartime jobs so that men returning from war could fill them. Although over 25 percent of American women remained in the workforce, women in the late 1940s, 1950s, and 1960s were expected to seek marriage and motherhood, not careers. Women who chose to remain single or who took their careers seriously were seen as unfeminine. Married women who worked were expected to quit their jobs if they became pregnant—and if they didn't, they were fired.

In 1963, President Kennedy's **Commission on the Status of Women** released findings that showed that women faced significant barriers in all aspects of their lives. The 1963 **Equal Pay Act** made paying women less than men for the same work illegal. However, the law was ineffective because it allowed employers to claim reasons other than gender for paying women less than men. In 1978, the **Pregnancy Discrimination Act** made it illegal to discriminate against or fire employees who became pregnant.

In 1966, **Barbara Jordan** became the first African American woman to serve in the Texas State Legislature. Ten years later, she spoke at the Democratic National Convention in support of Jimmy Carter; this made her the first black woman to speak on behalf of a presidential candidate in a national setting. Her speech, in which she discusses the meaning of American democracy to the poor and disenfranchised, has appeared on SAT READING.

Title VII: This section of the 1964 Civil Rights Act prohibits employment discrimination on the basis of race, color, sex, religion, or national origin, although loopholes in the Equal Pay Act initially limited its effectiveness. For example, jobs that were performed primarily by women, such as teaching, secretarial work, childcare, and nursing were judged to be less skilled and less important than jobs done by men. It also said that employers could not refuse to hire women with young children if they hired men who had children of the same age. Later court cases established that it was illegal for employers to advertise jobs as specifically for one sex only.

Title IX: In 1972, the federal government passed Title IX of the **Education Amendments Act** to extend the protections of the 1964 Civil Rights Act (above) to female athletes. Biographies of female athletes who overcame barriers of sex or race have appeared on **SAT WRITING**.

Native American Rights Movement: Since the 1880s, it had been official United States policy to assimilate (absorb) Native Americans into American society. Native Americans had been granted United States citizenship in 1924*, but they were often prevented from voting. They lived in extreme poverty with inadequate nutrition, poor health care, and overcrowded schools. Large portions of their land had been sold to white Americans. The government tried to weaken tribal identity by requiring Native children to live in boarding schools far from their homes, where they were expected to look, speak, and act like white children, speaking only English and observing Christian holidays instead of Native ones.

> * The 1886 **Fourteenth Amendment** excluded Native Americans from United States citizenship.

Indian Relocation Act of 1956: This Act was also known as the **Indian Termination Act** because it was designed to terminate (kill) Native American tribal identity by destroying the legal existence of the tribes themselves and assimilating (absorbing) individual Natives into American society. Lengthy court battles ensued (followed), but many Natives sold their land on the reservations and relocated to cities, where they were subject to racial discrimination and police brutality.

Native rights groups conducted dramatic protests to draw attention to their claims of stolen land, and the policy of tribal termination ended with the 1968 **Indian Civil Rights Act.** In 1969, Native rights activists occupied Alcatraz Island, a former federal prison, because they wanted to reclaim the land. In 1970, activists occupied Plymouth Rock in Massachusetts and Mount Rushmore, the South Dakota mountain that bears the sculptures of four American presidents, to draw attention to the theft of Native land and the poor treatment that Natives Americans had suffered at the hands of the United States government.

Trail of Broken Treaties: In 1972, over seven hundred activists from twenty-five states participated in a cross-country march that ended with a six-day occupation of the **Bureau of Indian Affairs** in Washington, DC, to demand new, enforceable land treaties to replace those that had been broken. In 1978, another cross-country march demanded an end to the lack of resources and high poverty that plagued Native American communities.

Native American history appears on SAT READING in the form of speeches by presidents and tribal leaders and in literature passages from novels by Native authors such as **Louise Erdrich, Les-**

lie Marmon Silko, N. Scott Momaday, Sherman Alexie, and Mary Brave Bird. SAT WRITING has included passages about the lives of important Native Americans.

Chicano Rights: Some Americans of Mexican descent refer to themselves as *Chicano* (for males) or *Chicana* (for females). In the 1960s and 1970s, Chicano and Chicana activists formed *El Movimiento* (the Movement) to combat prejudice against *La Raza* (the Race) and advocate for fuller inclusion in American society. Members of El Movimiento rejected the idea that they should look and act white and identified instead with African Americans' struggle for racial equality. Many Mexican Americans worked as migrant farm workers, suffering low pay, poor working conditions, and no job security. The **United Farm Workers** leaders **Dolores Huerta** and **Cesar Chavez** led national boycotts on grapes and lettuce to win better pay and safer working conditions for farm workers. Their stories, as well as passages about El Movimiento's public art projects, have appeared in SAT WRITING passages.

The Gay Rights Movement: In the mid-twentieth century, people who were LGBTQ+ knew that they had to keep their identities secret. In 1952, homosexuality was labelled a mental illness by the **American Psychiatric Association**. In 1953, President Eisenhower banned "sexual deviants" from holding federal jobs. People who were LGBTQ+ were denied housing, fired from their jobs, and refused service in restaurants and bars. In fact, restaurants and bars could be closed by city and town governments simply for serving LGBTQ+ people.

However, bars and restaurants served an important social function in the LGBTQ+ community, many of whose members were estranged (cut off) from their families and had few places where they could socialize with others like themselves. In New York City, the **Stonewall Inn** was among one of the many bars that catered to the LGBTQ+ community, surviving despite repeated police efforts to close them down.

On June 28, 1969, the Stonewall was raided by police for operating without a liquor license and for serving LGBTQ+ customers. They arrested its employees and customers they thought were cross-dressing* as members of the opposite sex and told everyone else to go home. People were angry, however, because there had been two other raids recently. Instead of obeying, they shouted insults and threw bottles and other objects at the police as they loaded their prisoners into a van. Police at the scene radioed for reinforcements and barricaded themselves in the bar, but the protestors broke through the barricade. In the ensuing melee (fight), the police threw tear gas, and someone set the bar on fire. A few police officers were injured, but none seriously.

> * Today, many people assume that all **transvestites** (crossdressers) are biological males who dress as women, but back then, women could also be arrested for having short hair, not wearing makeup, or for dressing in jeans and a T-shirt. Some of the people the police arrested at the Stonewall Inn on the night of the riot were biological women whose appearance the police saw as "unfeminine."

The next day, the Stonewall opened for business, despite its burned bar, broken furniture, and broken doors. It did not serve alcohol because it had no liquor license, but customers began arriving anyway. Many of them were gay rights activists who connected their struggles with those of African Americans, women, and other minority groups, and the events at the inn became a symbol of LGBTQ+ solidarity and resistance to oppression. When activists held the first **gay rights parade** on the one-year anniversary of the uprising, they began their march at the Stonewall Inn.

The End of the Cold War (1980–1991)

The 1970s were a period of relative calm in the Cold War. The Soviet Union and the United States expanded trade with each other and negotiated several treaties that limited the number and type of nuclear weapons that each could have. At the same time, however, postcolonial revolutions and unrest in Asia, the Middle East, and Central America escalated Cold War tensions as the United States and Soviet Union each tried to influence events in their favor.

Soviet Union Invades Afghanistan: Afghanistan is a landlocked (without sea access) Asian country that shares borders with both Iran and Pakistan. It has been an officially Muslim state since the end of the nineteenth century.

In 1978, after several years of political and economic instability, the communist **People's Democratic Party of Afghanistan (PDPA)** overthrew the government and seized power. It invited the Soviet Union to train its army and help improve its infrastructure. The PDPA also ruthlessly suppressed all opposition, arresting, torturing, and killing thousands. It discouraged religious observance, closed mosques, required men to cut their beards*, and banned the *chador*, a traditional garment that covers women from head to toe. These policies were extremely unpopular, and armed resistance groups sprang up throughout the country.

> ✳ Beards are seen as a sign of faith for Muslim men.

Conflict between factions within the PDPA worsened Afghanistan's turmoil. In 1979, its leader was assassinated by his second-in-command. The Soviet Union thought that the new leader would be anti-communist and pro-United States, so it invaded and installed a new pro-Soviet leader.

Many Muslim nations saw the Soviet invasion as an attack on Islam, and thousands of Muslims from other countries joined the *mujahideen* (Muslim fighters) against the Soviet invaders. Many countries, including the United States, funded these fighters, and Pakistan allowed *mujahideen* forces to train in unpopulated areas along its border with Afghanistan.

Reagan Doctrine: President Reagan believed that the Soviet invasion of Afghanistan indicated a growing communist threat, and he responded with a statement that became known as the **Reagan Doctrine:** "We must not break faith with those who are risking their lives ... on every continent, from Afghanistan to Nicaragua ... to defy Soviet aggression and secure rights which have been ours from birth. Support for freedom fighters is self-defense." Many historians believe that the Reagan Doctrine helped the United States win the Cold War.

Changes in the Soviet Union: When **Mikhail Gorbachev** became the leader of the Soviet Union in 1985, he introduced a series of reforms that were intended to overcome the inefficiency of the Soviet economy. His ideas are referred to as *glasnost* (openness) and *perestroika* (restructuring).

Perestroika meant that farmers and manufacturers were now free to decide what to produce and how much to charge for it. Restrictions were loosened so that Russian businesses could sell their products internationally. However, *perestroika* also caused shortages and created dissatisfaction throughout the Soviet Union. Workers demanded higher wages, and this set off a spiral of inflation that made Soviet money less valuable, which in turn meant that food and other items became more unaffordable for many.

At the same time, the policy of *glasnost* meant that government records that had been hidden for decades were opened. There was now freedom of the press, so Soviet citizens learned about Soviet mistakes, atrocities, and cover-ups for the first time. People were angry, and as the economy worsened, they staged anti-government protests. Unlike previous leaders of the Soviet Union, Gorbachev chose not to send the Soviet military to quell (stop) unrest, and this decision set in motion the chain of events that led to his government's collapse.

Fall of the Berlin Wall: As conditions worsened in the Soviet Union, Gorbachev and Reagan negotiated a series of treaties in 1987 that removed all intermediate-range nuclear weapons in Europe.

President Reagan capitalized on that success in a speech he made during a 1989 visit to West Berlin in which he demanded, "Mr. Gorbachev, tear down this wall." Since this is probably Reagan's most famous speech, it is a good candidate for an SAT READING passage.

The Berlin Wall was built in 1961 (above) to prevent East Germans from fleeing to West Germany. As West Berlin enjoyed the prosperity and freedom of Western Europe, East Berlin became poorer, shabbier, and more totalitarian. In November 1989, East Berlin officials, for the first time, approved a permit for a political protest. During the protest, an official announced that any East German citizen who wanted to leave East Germany was now free to do so. Jubilant (joyful) crowds gathered on both sides of the Berlin Wall, drinking and celebrating. When the gates opened at midnight, thousands of East Germans surged through the gates. A two-day street party began as East German citizens reunited with family and friends and celebrated their new freedom. The wall was torn down in the days that followed.

Poland and the Solidarity Movement: In 1980, the communist Polish government allowed **Solidarity**, the country's first legally recognized labor union, to form. The leaders of the Polish military responded by declaring martial law and arresting hundreds of Solidarity leaders. Military rule ended in 1984, and those who had been jailed were freed. In 1989, negotiations between Solidarity and the Polish government resulted in a multiparty election in which the state Communist Party was defeated. Solidarity's leader, **Lech Walesa**, became president, and Poland transitioned to a capitalist economy. Walesa was awarded the 1983 Nobel Peace Prize for his leadership of the Solidarity Movement. His acceptance speech could be on SAT READING.

The Estonian Singing Revolution (1986–1991): The Baltic Republic of Estonia lies between Russia and the Baltic Sea. It was absorbed into the Soviet Union in 1940, and large segments of its population were forcibly deported to Siberia, the coldest, least developed region of the Soviet Union. Estonia lost about one-fourth of its population to deportation, imprisonment, and execution. Its flag, language, and music were forbidden, and Russian became its official language.

Estonians responded to the liberalizing (freeing) effects of *glasnost* and *perestroika* (openness and restructuring) by testing the limits of these policies. Beginning in 1987, large musical events took place in which crowds of thousands held hands and sang banned patriotic music. Such events became popular as did the singing of patriotic songs at anti-Russian protests. The largest mass singing event included about 300,000 people—about one-fourth of Estonia's total population—and took place in Tallinn, Estonia's capital city, in 1988. Passages about the **Tallinn Music Festival** have been on **SAT READING**.

The August Coup (August 1991): Although *glasnost* and *perestroika* were popular with individual Soviet citizens, many within the Soviet government and military opposed Gorbachev's policies as a threat to Soviet authoritarian rule.

On August 18, Gorbachev was vacationing at his estate in Ukraine when a group of government and military officials arrived, cut the telephone lines, and isolated him from the outside world. News outlets announced that he had resigned due to illness, and coup participants raced to Moscow to seize control of the government. However, **Russian President Boris Yeltsin*** denounced (publicly opposed) the coup. Under his leadership, protestors barricaded city streets with trolley cars and city buses or formed human chains to block Soviet tanks.

> * Yeltsin was the president of Russia while it was still part of the Soviet Union. Gorbachev was the president of the Soviet Union.

The coup leaders were unprepared for such widespread opposition. When some military units refused to follow orders and instead sided with Gorbachev's supporters, they realized that they had failed. They were arrested and Gorbachev regained control of the country.

Celebrating protesters decorated Soviet tanks with
flowers in the protests against the 1991 August Coup.

In the months following the unsuccessful coup, independence movements flourished throughout the Soviet Union because Gorbachev, unlike the Soviet leaders who preceded him, did not order military action to quell them. By the end of the year, the largest single country in the world had fractured into fifteen independent nations*. In a speech that declared, "The Cold War is over," Gorbachev resigned on December 25, 1991, and the Soviet Union—after seventy years—ceased to exist.

*   Armenia, Azerbaijan, Belarus, Estonia, Georgia, Kazakhstan, Kyrgyzstan, Latvia, Lithuania, Moldova, Russia, Tajikistan, Turkmenistan, Ukraine, and Uzbekistan.

PART III: POST-COLD WAR TO THE END OF HISTORY ACCORDING TO THE SAT (1991–1995)

Globalization

The fall of the Soviet Union meant that the world was no longer divided into two opposing camps, and this new geopolitical reality created optimistic predictions that **globalization** (the growth of international economic, cultural, and political networks) could remake and perfect the world. SAT READING and SAT WRITING frequently include passages about how globalization has affected health care, climate change, education, and poverty.

South Africa and Apartheid

The struggle of black South Africans against its system of **apartheid** (racial segregation) captured the world's attention in the 1980s.

South Africa was colonized by two European groups—the Boers and the British—who fought the Boer Wars (above) between 1899 and 1902. The British won.

In 1910, four British colonies* united to form the **Union of South Africa**, a self-governing nation within the larger British Empire. It was governed by white South Africans who divided South Africa into four racial groups: whites, Asians, "coloreds,"** and blacks, with black people at the bottom. Only white people were allowed to vote.

> * Cape Colony, Natal, Transvaal, and the Orange Free State.

> ** People of mixed race.

In 1948, South Africa's all-white government created the apartheid system to limit the economic and educational opportunities of non-white South Africans and to police every aspect of their lives.

In 1950, the apartheid government passed the **Population Registration Act**, the first in a series of repressive laws. All black South Africans over the age of sixteen were required to carry a "passbook" that contained their name, identity number, fingerprints, and picture, as well as details about their employment that determined where they were allowed to be. Those caught without their passbooks could be arrested and jailed, often far from their homes and families. This practice regularly left black children without their caretakers.

Other laws forbade interracial marriage and sexual relationships. Comedian **Trevor Noah's** 2016 memoir, *Born a Crime: Stories* *from a South African Childhood,* points out that when he was born in 1984, his very existence was against the law.

Racial segregation in apartheid South Africa.

Defiance Campaign: Black South Africans immediately began organizing to resist apartheid. In 1952, the **African National Congress (ANC)** began a nonviolent **Defiance Campaign.** The campaign asked black protesters to use facilities that were marked "whites only" and to refuse to carry their passbooks. Within six months, over eight thousand people had been arrested, mostly for nonviolent misdemeanors (small crimes) like sitting on a "whites only" bench or entering a train station through the wrong door. Speeches by ANC members who opposed apartheid have appeared on SAT READING, sometimes paired with passages by white South African government officials.

Nelson Mandela (1918–2013): Nelson* Mandela was born into a royal family among the Thembu, a Xhosa-speaking people whose traditional lands were part of South Africa. His upbringing included attendance at the most exclusive schools for black South Africans.

* Mandela's parents named him "Rolihlahla," which means "Troublemaker" in Xhosa, but the all-black

> elementary school he attended renamed him Nelson because its policy was that all children were to be given "Christian" first names.

Sharpeville Massacre (1960): South African police shot into a crowd of about two hundred fifty peaceful black protesters. Sixty-nine were killed and over one hundred were injured. Mandela was among the thousands who were arrested in the massacre's aftermath, but he was released shortly afterwards. The South African government outlawed the ANC, which went underground (began working in secret), organized a general labor strike, and cooperated with the **South African Communist Party** to form *Umkhonto we Sizwe** **(known as MK)**, an armed group dedicated to sabotaging (deliberately destroying) government facilities and infrastructure.

* | Xhosa for "Spear of the Nation."

Mandela was one of MK's founders and leaders. In 1962, he traveled illegally to a conference in Ethiopia and was arrested and jailed for leaving the country without a permit when he returned to South Africa.

Rivonia Trial (1963–1964): Mandela went on trial with a number of other MK leaders. They were charged with sabotage, assisting South Africa's enemies, and furthering communism*. Excerpts from Mandela's three-hour-long **"Speech from the Dock**,"** also known as **"Why I Am Prepared to Die,"** has appeared on SAT READING. In it, Mandela explains that the ANC abandoned its belief in nonviolence because the Sharpeville Massacre showed that "the government intended to rule by force alone." He also says, "the African people were not part of the government and did not make the laws by which they were governed," and that "for us to accept the banning [of the ANC] was equivalent to accepting the silencing of the African people for all time."

> * | The Cold War was at its height in the early 1960s. The apartheid government opposed communism because it feared that a communist regime would abolish racial segregation.

> * * | A defendant's seat (or place to stand) while court is in session.

Mandela received a sentence of life imprisonment, as did his codefendants. Three others were condemned to death by hanging and the one white defendant was sent to an all-white prison.

Soweto Youth Uprising (1976): Twenty thousand schoolchildren missed school to protest the government's decision to require black South Africans to learn Afrikaans* as well as English in school. South African police fired into the crowd and as many as seven hundred children died. This incident caused an international outcry that energized the global anti-apartheid campaign.

> * | Afrikaans evolved from Dutch and was spoken by white South Africans.

This photograph became an icon (symbol) of the Soweto Uprising.

Divestment: British and American students began protesting apartheid during the 1960s, but they had no influence over the South African government. They decided to pressure their colleges and universities to divest (sell) any investments they had in companies that did business in South Africa*. The students hoped that divestment would weaken South Africa's economy and harm its global reputation.

> * Colleges and universities make a lot of money by investing in the stock market.

The divestment campaign took over a decade to gather support, but the international community showed its disapproval of apartheid in other ways. For example, South Africa was not permitted to compete in the **1964 Olympics** because it refused to send racially mixed teams. In 1970 a number of countries withdrew from the international **Chess Olympiad** to protest South Africa's inclusion. Albania withdrew even though that meant it forfeited (lost by not playing) its match with South Africa. Other sports, including golf, cricket, and tennis, experienced disruption when individual players and international associations refused to compete against South African athletes. Passages about international sports during the apartheid era could appear on SAT WRITING.

By the 1980s, black South African resistance to apartheid had escalated significantly, and media coverage of the unrest gave new momentum to the divestment campaign. American students continued to advocate for divestment, and by 1990, American investors had withdrawn about one billion dollars from the South African economy.

In 1989, **F. W. de Klerk** became the leader of the apartheid government. He believed that South Africa would break apart unless apartheid ended. He lifted the bans on black nationalist groups, restored freedom of the press and freed Mandela and many other political prisoners. He and Mandela then negotiated the terms under which South Africa would transition from a segregated police state into a well-integrated multiracial democracy.

In 1993, de Klerk announced a national election in which people of all races could vote for members of the South African parliament, and in 1994, the now racially mixed government elected Mandela as the first president of post-apartheid South Africa. Mandela and de Klerk were jointly awarded the 1993 Nobel Peace Prize. Their speeches could appear on SAT READING.

HIV/AIDS

Human Immunodeficiency Virus (HIV) is the virus that causes Acquired Immunodeficiency Syndrome (AIDS). Scientists think that a variant of the virus was transmitted from chimpanzees to people who hunted them for food and that it was probably spreading slowly in the United States by the early 1970s. By

1981, it had been identified as the cause of sudden clusters of similar illnesses in otherwise healthy young homosexual men. By 1983, cases had also appeared among intravenous drug users, hemophiliacs*, and Haitians. In the eyes of the American public, only hemophiliacs were worthy of help or compassion.

> * People whose blood does not clot. Hemophiliacs often require blood transfusions after sustaining even minor injuries.

AIDS quickly became known as the "gay disease." The fear of being perceived as gay or gay-friendly slowed the governmental response to the new epidemic. President Ronald Reagan did not mention AIDS in public until 1985 after more than five thousand Americans had already died from it. Some religious leaders declared that HIV/AIDS was "God's punishment" for immoral behavior. Similar prejudice faced people who contracted the virus after injecting illegal drugs. Many people with AIDS lost their homes and jobs because people were afraid of catching it from them. Some hospitals refused to treat AIDS patients.

In 1984, **Ryan White**, a thirteen-year-old from Indiana, became infected with HIV/AIDS after receiving a blood transfusion for his hemophilia. Despite assurances from doctors that the disease was not airborne, and that White did not pose a danger to other students, many parents and teachers opposed his return to school. Even after he was allowed to return, he was barred from taking gym and required to eat with disposable utensils and use a separate bathroom.

White's struggle to attend school received a lot of media coverage, and he came to represent "innocent" AIDS victims who did not contract their disease by engaging in "immoral" behavior.

He appeared regularly on television to combat prejudice against people with HIV/AIDS until his death in 1990. A few months later, Congress passed the **Ryan White Comprehensive AIDS Resources Emergency (CARE) Act**, a federally funded program to provide medical care to people with HIV/AIDS who are uninsured or underinsured.

Basketball superstar **Magic Johnson** also challenged the stereotype that HIV/AIDS only affected gay white men when he, a heterosexual African American, announced his positive diagnosis and retirement* from basketball in a 1991 press conference that made headlines around the world. He became an outspoken critic of the government's response to the epidemic and has helped to raise millions of dollars for AIDS prevention and drug treatment programs.

> *   Johnson returned to play with his team, the Los Angeles Lakers, and was named "Most Valuable Player" in 1992.

When **President George H. W. Bush** was elected in 1988, he continued Reagan's mostly hands-off AIDS policy. However, as the number of deaths rose, anger grew at the government's seeming indifference to the health crisis.

In 1991, the **AIDS Coalition to Unleash Power (ACT UP)** staged numerous protests around the country because government funding for AIDS research had decreased despite the rapid spread of the virus throughout the country. During Bush's 1992 reelection campaign, activists dumped the ashes of their dead friends and loved ones on the White House lawn. In another protest, they brought the body of an AIDS activist to President Bush's reelection headquarters in New York City.

ACT UP protesters raising a banner to protest government inaction during the 1991 "**Day of Desperation.**"

As public pressure to improve the government's response to the epidemic continued, President Bush's reelection committee invited **Mary Fisher**, a lifelong Republican and personal friend of the Bush family, to speak at the Republican National Convention about her own AIDS diagnosis. In the speech, which has been used for SAT READING, Fisher says she intends to "lift the shroud (cover) of silence" that prevents people from discussing AIDS in public. She portrays the president as a compassionate friend during a dark time and urges her audience to remember that no one is immune from the virus. Fisher's speech was an enormous success and she went on to become a vocal AIDS activist. For reasons unrelated to Fisher's speech, President Bush did not win reelection.

"Women's Rights are Human Rights"

In 1995, almost fifty thousand people from 189 countries gathered in Beijing, China, to participate in the United Nations' **Fourth World Conference on Women**. The conference's goal was to ratify (approve) the **Beijing Declaration and Platform for Action**, a document that listed "strategic objectives" in twelve areas* in which the universal human rights of women are abridged (lessened) or denied.

> * Women and poverty; education and training of women; women and health; violence against women; women and armed conflict; women and the economy; women in power and decision-making; mechanisms for the advancement of women; human rights of women; women and the media; women and the environment; and the girl child.

American **First Lady Hillary Clinton** was invited to speak at the Beijing conference, and her speech has appeared on SAT READING. It emphasizes the many ways that women contribute to the well-being of their families and communities and urges that world leaders listen to what women have to say. After listing some of the ways that girls and women are denied their human rights, Clinton says, "If there is one message that echoes forth from this conference, let it be that human rights are women's rights and women's rights are human rights once and for all."

CONCLUSION

Many students seem to experience history as a series of isolated, unconnected events, and this often causes them to make mistakes that more knowledgeable test-takers avoid. I wrote this book to share the background knowledge I have about the causes and consequences of ideologies, inventions, revolutions, conquests, and wars. The book will also help you connect the dates in explanatory notes on SAT READING to relevant background knowledge that makes it easier to select the correct answers to questions about a passage's main idea, primary purpose, and its references and allusions.

SAT WRITING questions also test reading comprehension, even though the questions are asked from a grammatical perspective. Questions about whether sentences should be added, deleted, or revised and questions that ask you to select the best topic sentence for a paragraph or to match main ideas with the most relevant details are really testing your ability to determine main idea and primary purpose and your ability to read contextually. For example, knowing that Joseph Stalin was a harsh dictator gives you contextual information for passages about the struggles of Soviet dissidents and makes it less likely that you will be fooled into selecting an off-topic detail to match the passage's main idea.

Ending with Hillary Clinton's "Women's Rights are Human Rights" speech was unplanned, but it underscores just how central the ideas of democracy and universal human rights are to the SAT and the way that it presents American history. I also didn't set out to become a more committed believer in American democracy, but the ideals expressed in the United States' founding documents (and all the others) have convinced me that Winston Churchill was right when he said, "No one pretends that democracy is perfect or all-wise. Indeed, it has been said that democracy is the worst form of government except for all those other forms that have been tried from time to time."

IMAGE ATTRIBUTIONS

Thanks to the following sources for providing images.

British Isles map, pg. 15 – Panther Media GmbH / Alamy Stock
Mona Lisa, pg. 26 – GiorgioMorara - stock.adobe.com
The Last Supper, pg. 26 – Renáta Sedmáková - stock.adobe.com
Michelangelo's David, pg. 27 – Livioandronico2013, CC BY-SA 4.0, via Wikimedia Commons
Sistine Chapel ceiling, pg. 27 – photogolfer - stock.adobe.com
Istanbul land bridge map, pg. 31 – Peter Hermes Furian - stock.adobe.com
Triangle Trade map, pg. 36 – arkela - stock.adobe.com
Thirteen Colonies map, pg. 42 – Anadolu_Dizgi/Shutterstock.com
Washington Crosses the Delaware, pg. 48 – Art Collection / Alamy Stock Photo
Flying shuttle, pg. 54 – Juulijs - stock.adobe.com
Spinning wheel, pg. 54 – Kate Smith - stock.adobe.com
Spinning jenny, pg. 54 – Juulijs - stock.adobe.com
Cotton gin, pg. 55 – PK Designs/Shutterstock.com
First steam engine, pg. 56 – FLHC 1C / Alamy Stock Photo
Oldest photo, pg. 57 – Joseph Nicéphore Niépce, Public domain, via Wikimedia Commons
Two guillotines, pg. 66 – Yogi Black / Alamy Stock Photo
Hispaniola map, pg. 68 – Peter Hermes Furian - stock.adobe.com
Louisiana purchase map, pg. 78 – IanDagnall Computing / Alamy Stock Photo
Uncle Sam, pg. 80 – Bettmann via Getty Images
Manifest Destiny, pg. 84 – Public domain via Library of Congress
Missouri Compromise map, pg. 88 – stock.adobe.com, SPS
Kansans-Missouri map, pg. 89 – pavalena - stock.adobe.com
Confederate states map, pg. 94 – Ingo Menhard - stock.adobe.com
General Order No. 3, pg. 97 – Science History Images / Alamy Stock Photo
Sherman's March map, pg. 101 – ad_hominem - stock.adobe.com

Incarcerated black children, pg. 105 – Everett Collection/Shutterstock.com

Plessy v. Ferguson newspaper article, pg. 107 – Public domain via Library of Congress

Wanted ad, pg. 109 – FLHC26 / Alamy Stock Photo

Magic Washer poster, pg. 110 – Public domain via Library of Congress

Carpet sweeper ad, pg. 113 – Hera Vintage Ads / Alamy Stock Photo

Jacob Riis immigrant photo, pg. 116 – Jacob Riis, Lodgers in a Crowded Bayard Street Tenement, Created: 1 January 1889, Public domain via Wikimedia Commons

Temperance women photo, pg. 119 – Smith Archive / Alamy Stock Photo

Haymarket Square Riot illustration, pg. 120 – Public domain via Library of Congress

George Pullman cartoon, pg. 121 – Chicago Labor Newspaper, July 7, 1894., Public domain, via Wikimedia Commons

1914 map of Europe, pg. 124 – Robert R Condon - stock.adobe.com, SPS

Lusitania warning, pg. 127 – Unknown author, Public domain, via Wikimedia Commons

1914 vs. 1918 Middle East Map, pg. 131 – Maxim Grebeshkov - stock.adobe.com, SPS

Europe before and after WWI map, pg. 132 – Robert R Condon - stock.adobe.com, Jelle Wesseling via iStock, SPS

NAACP flag photo, pg. 136 – JJs / Alamy Stock Photo

Miguel Covarrubias cartoon, pg. 137 – Retro AdArchives / Alamy Stock Photo

L'Aveu difficile, pg. 141 – The History Collection / Alamy Stock Photo

Chrysler Building photo, pg. 141 – "Chrysler Building tower in Manhattan. Original image from Carol M. Highsmith's America, Library of Congress collection. Digitally enhanced by rawpixel." by Carol M Highsmith is marked with CC0 1.0.

Art Deco fonts, pg. 141 – SPS

Im Blau, pg. 141 – The Artchives / Alamy Stock Photo

Dr. Seuss cartoon, pg. 151 – GRANGER

Map of Poland, pg. 153 – Markoff - stock.adobe.com, SPS

1942 map of Europe, pg. 155 – P.J. Mode collection of persuasive cartography, #8548. Division of Rare and Manuscript Collections, Cornell University Library.

Operation Barbarossa map, pg. 157 – Peter Hermes Furian - stock.adobe.com

Empire of Japan map, pg. 157 – Dimitrios - stock.adobe.com, SPS

Don't Waste Food poster, pg. 161 – Public domain via Library of Congress

Service on the Home Front poster, pg. 161 - WPA poster by Louis Hirshman, via Library of Congress website, Public Domain

This is the Enemy poster, pg. 162 – Retro AdArchives / Alamy Stock Photo

Photo of Japanese family, pg. 163 – ASSOCIATED PRESS

Rosie the Riveter poster, pg. 164 – J. Howard Miller (1918–2004), artist employed by Westinghouse, poster used by the War Production Co-ordinating Committee - From scan of copy belonging to the National Museum of American History, Smithsonian Institution, retrieved from the website of the Virginia Historical Society.

Double V logo, pg. 167 – Pittsburgh Courier Archives

North Africa map, pg. 168 – PJF Military Collection / Alamy Stock Photo

German concentration camps map, pg. 173 – ad_hominem - stock.adobe.com

1947 Partition of India map, pg. 178 – negoworks - stock.adobe.com, SPS

Dispute over Kashmir map, pg. 178 – Tupungato - stock.adobe.com

Ancient Palestine map, pg. 180 – Itan1409 - stock.adobe.com

Israel before and after Six-Day War map, pg. 186 – Olli - stock.adobe.com, SPS

Western Europe vs. Soviet Union map, pg. 192 – Gerhard Egger - stock.adobe.com

Dominoes image, pg. 193 – viperagp - stock.adobe.com

Lavender Scare protest, pg. 197 – Photo by Bettmann via Getty Images

Germany 1945-90 map, pg. 199 – bitmedia.dk - stock.adobe.com

LBJ swearing in photo, pg. 203 – This file is a work of an employee of the Executive Office of the President of the United States, taken or made as part of that person's official duties. As a work of the U.S. federal government, it is in the public domain.

LBJ protest photo, pg. 208 – Photo by Clive Limpkin/Express/Hulton Archive/ Getty Images

Rotary handset photo, pg. 212 – michaklootwijk - stock.adobe.com

Vietnamese "boat people" photo, pg. 215 – This file is a work of a sailor or employee of the U.S. Navy, taken or made as part of that person's official duties. As a work of the U.S. federal government, it is in the public domain in the United States.

Bus burning photo, pg. 220 – Photo by Bettmann via Getty Images

Fire hosing protesters photo, pg. 221 – Black Star / Alamy Stock Photo

Angela Davis photo, pg. 229 – Science History Images / Alamy Stock Photo

August Coup protest photo, pg. 241 – Photo by Peter Turnley/Corbis/VCG via Getty Images

Train station in South Africa photo, pg. 245 – Franz Aberham via Getty Images

Soweto Uprising photo, pg. 248 – Photo by Gideon Mendel/Corbis via Getty Images

ACT UP protesters photo, pg. 252 – Photo by Dirck Halstead/Getty Images

ACKNOWLEDGMENTS

Many thanks to Dan Breau, Sylvia Breau, Mike Hoffman, Meagan Hoffman, Seth Rigberg, Susan Kheel, and Alan Cooper for the time and effort they put into reading and commenting on the various drafts of this book. Much appreciation also goes to Adolfo Aaron for his patience, encouragement, and support throughout the writing process.

ABOUT THE AUTHOR

Dr. Breau double-majored in history and English as an undergraduate at Rutgers University before completing her graduate work at Vanderbilt University. She has taught grades 7-12 as well as numerous college classes. She was a co-recipient of the 2008 College Board Bob Costas Award for Excellence in the Teaching of Writing for her role in a student publication. She has published scholarly articles, book reviews, including many about history books, and lifestyle articles, one of which appears in *Chicken Soup for the Divorced Soul*. *History According to SAT* is her first book.